WONG KAR-WAI'S
Happy
Together

T0345753

Hong Kong University Press thanks Xu Bing for writing the Press's name in his Square Word Calligraphy for the covers of its books. For further information see p. iv.

THE NEW HONG KONG CINEMA SERIES

Series General Editors

Ackbar Abbas
Wimal Dissanayake
Mette Hjort
Gina Marchetti
Stephen Teo

Series Advisors

Chris Berry
Nick Browne
Ann Hui
Leo Lee
Li Cheuk-to
Patricia Mellencamp
Meaghan Morris
Paul Willemen
Peter Wollen
Wu Hung

✦ ✦ ✦ ✦ ✦

WONG KAR-WAI'S
Happy Together

Jeremy Tambling

香港大學出版社
HONG KONG UNIVERSITY PRESS

Hong Kong University Press
14/F Hing Wai Centre
7 Tin Wan Praya Road
Aberdeen
Hong Kong

© Hong Kong University Press 2003

Hardback edition first published 2003
Paperback edition first published 2003, reprinted 2006

Hardback   ISBN-13 978-962-209-588-5
             ISBN-10 962-209-588-7
Paperback ISBN-13 978-962-209-589-2
             ISBN-10 962-209-589-5

British Library Cataloguing-in-Publication Data
A catalogue record for this book is available from the British Library.

Secure on-line Ordering
http://www.hkupress.org

Printed and bound by Condor Production Ltd., Hong Kong, China

Hong Kong University Press is honoured that Xu Bing, whose art
explores the complex themes of language across cultures, has
written the Press's name in his Square Word Calligraphy. This
signals our commitment to cross-cultural thinking and the
distinctive nature of our English-language books published in
China.

"At first glance, Square Word Calligraphy appears to be nothing
more unusual than Chinese characters, but in fact it is a new way of
rendering English words in the format of a square so they resemble
Chinese characters. Chinese viewers expect to be able to read Square
Word Calligraphy but cannot. Western viewers, however are
surprised to find they can read it. Delight erupts when meaning is
unexpectedly revealed."

— Britta Erickson, *The Art of Xu Bing*

Contents

Series Preface

The New Hong Kong cinema came into existence under very special circumstances, during a period of social and political crisis resulting in a change of cultural paradigms. Such critical moments have produced the cinematic achievements of the early Soviet cinema, neorealism, the *nouvelle vague*, the German cinema in the 1970s and, we can now say, the recent Hong Kong cinema. If this cinema grew increasingly intriguing in the 1980s, after the announcement of Hong Kong's return to China, it was largely because it had to confront a new cultural and political space that was both complex and hard to define, where the problems of colonialism were overlaid with those of globalism in an uncanny way. Such uncanniness could not be caught through straight documentary or conventional history writing; it was left to the cinema to define it.

It does so by presenting to us an urban space that slips away if we try to grasp it too directly, a space that cinema coaxes into existence by whatever means at its disposal. Thus it is by eschewing a narrow idea of relevance and pursuing disreputable genres like melodrama, kung fu and the fantastic that cinema brings into view something else about the city which could otherwise be missed.

One classic example is Stanley Kwan's *Rouge*, which draws on the unrealistic form of the ghost story to evoke something of the uncanniness of Hong Kong's urban space. It takes a ghost to catch a ghost.

In the new Hong Kong cinema, then, it is neither the subject matter nor a particular set of generic conventions that is paramount. In fact, many Hong Kong films begin by following generic conventions but proceed to transform them. Such transformation of genre is also the transformation of a sense of place where all the rules have quietly and deceptively changed. It is this shifting sense of place, often expressed negatively and indirectly — but in the best work always rendered precisely in (necessarily) innovative images — that is decisive for the New Hong Kong Cinema.

Has the creative period of the New Hong Kong Cinema come to an end? However we answer the question, there is a need now to evaluate the achievements of Hong Kong cinema. During the last few years, a number of full-length books have appeared, testifying to the topicality of the subject. These books survey the field with varying degrees of success, but there is yet an almost complete lack of authoritative texts focusing in depth on individual Hong Kong films. This book series on the New Hong Kong Cinema is designed to fill this lack. Each volume will be written by a scholar/ critic who will analyse each chosen film in detail and provide a critical apparatus for further discussion including filmography and bibliography.

Our objective is to produce a set of interactional and provocative readings that would make a self-aware intervention into modern Hong Kong culture. We advocate no one theoretical position; the authors will approach their chosen films from their own distinct points of vantage and interest. The aim of the series is to generate open-ended discussions of the selected films, employing diverse analytical strategies, in order to urge the readers towards self-reflective engagements with the films in particular and the

Hong Kong cultural space in general. It is our hope that this series will contribute to the sharpening of Hong Kong culture's conceptions of itself.

In keeping with our conviction that film is not a self-enclosed signification system but an important cultural practice among similar others, we wish to explore how films both reflect and inflect culture. And it is useful to keep in mind that reflection of reality and realty of reflection are equally important in the understanding of cinema.

Ackbar Abbas
Wimal Dissanayake

Preface

I am grateful to Ackbar Abbas and Wimal Dissanayake, most supportive of colleagues, for the chance to write this book. A monograph on a single text is something I have always wanted to write but have never had the opportunity until now. My approach has been to draw on as many contexts as possible, thus there are many divagations into discussions of postcolonial theory and allegory derived from Walter Benjamin and Paul de Man in chapter 2, and discussions of Latin American and Argentinian novelists in chapter 3 — an interest first sparked in me by my then colleague, Jonathan Hall. These may possibly make the book look more 'literary' than expected, and perhaps less Hong Kong directed than some would like. I hope that my approach will nonetheless be found to be stimulating.

I am grateful to the Hong Kong University Press and especially Mina Kumar for taking on this project, and thankful to the anonymous readers of the Press who supplied many helpful points of criticism and of detail. I would also like to thank Block 2 Pictures Inc., for permission to reprint the film stills, and the Hong Kong Film Archive for providing the prints.

Above all, I would like to thank the students in the Department of Comparative Literature, always amongst the best in the University of Hong Kong, who have given me help or who have listened to me lecturing on *Happy Together* and taught me much more than they could possibly know. I refer to students doing 'The History of Sexuality' and to first-year students who attended my lectures on 'Gender Studies'. Several students have done MA or MPhil work which drew on Wong Kar-wai, and I would like to acknowledge Chan Yiu-hung, Patrick Suen Pak-kin, Ian Fong Ho-yin, Lo Wai-chun and Paul Kong, each of whom has given me ideas for this book. My thanks also go to Ho Cheuk-wing and Steven Pang for their help in translating Cantonese dialogue and my special thanks to Jamie Ku for preparing the bibliography. I would like to dedicate this book to all these Hong Kong students.

This book was written before the death of Leslie Cheung, and therefore pays tribute to the memory of a fine actor.

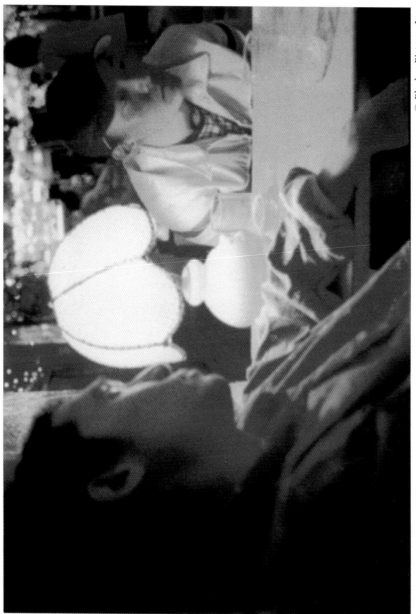

1

Introduction: Approaching the Film

In May 1997, just before Hong Kong passed from British colonial rule to the People's Republic of China — the event of June 30 which turned the colony into an S.A.R. (Special Administrative Region) — Hong Kong director Wong Kar-wai released the film *Happy Together* (春光乍洩). Wong Kar-wai was born in Shanghai in 1958 but he was brought up in Hong Kong and began film-making — if a beginning can be located at this point without being arbitrary about his previous work on films — with *As Tears Go By* (1988). This was a fast-paced gangland movie set in Kowloon which is frequently compared in plot with Martin Scorsese's *Mean Streets* (1973). It portrayed a gangster (Andy Lau) caught between the demands of his partner, Fly (Jacky Cheung), and his girlfriend (Maggie Cheung). As such, it can be seen as remaking a Hollywood formula, where the focus is on a male character proving his masculinity.[1]

Wong Kar-wai's second and more interesting film was *Days of Being Wild* (1990). Again, just as in *As Tears Go By*, the movie is set in Hong Kong and takes place in 1960. Capturing a moment gone or going by seems not only crucial to the film's director, but also to Yuddy (Leslie Cheung), the hero of the film who says to Maggie Cheung when she has told him the time, 'Because of you I'll remember this minute. From now on we've been friends for one minute.' The minute gains value because of the person, though the person may not last in the other's affection. Yuddy seems fully in control as shown most clearly in his relationships with his girlfriends (Maggie Cheung and Carina Lau) and the way in which he is the idol of his friend Zeb (Jacky Cheung). He is, however, consumed with a desire to know his mother who left him. Yuddy has been brought up by Rebecca (Rebecca Pan) who is about to emigrate to the USA in the same way that his first girlfriend is from Macau and seems likely to return there. Yuddy's sense of not having a secure place is increased when he journeys to the Philippines to find his mother. His quest ends in failure when she refuses to see him — meaning that the most important woman in his life refuses to validate him — and he dies at the hands of Filipino gangsters after having been robbed by a Filipina prostitute. The Philippines in this film has something of the quality of a mythical Wild West. This was the first Wong Kar-wai film that Australian photographer Chris Doyle worked on, relying mostly on a hand-held camera and following Wong Kar-wai in his technique of filming open-ended improvisations. Doyle has been associated with the director's films, except for *Fallen Angels,* ever since. Since Wong Kar-wai can hardly be said to work with a prewritten script — he films and then constructs the film largely on the cutting-room floor — collaboration, especially with Doyle, is essential in the making of his films.

His third film, *Ashes of Time* (1994), was derived from the martial-arts genre and set in mainland China but, again, had something of a western flavour to it. It compared two swordsmen, Ouyang Fang (Malevolent West) and Huang Yaoshi (Sinister East) and their parallel lives, although more time in the film is devoted to Ouyang Fang, the ascetic figure who wants to remember, as opposed to the womanizing Huang Yaoshi, a swordsman who wants to forget. Could these names be allegories for East and West, as these two bodies of geopolitical power impact on Hong Kong? I shall discuss this notion of allegory in the following chapter. The swordsmen were played by Leslie Cheung and Tony Leung Ka-fai. One of the film's heroes is the Blind Swordsman (Tony Leung Chiu-wai, the star of *Happy Together*) and another is the Shoeless Swordsman, Hong Qi (Jacky Cheung) — both figures of deprivation. Another kind of figure is the ambiguous character Murong Yang who is also Murong Yin (Brigitte Lin), first appearing in the movie in men's clothes. Maggie Cheung played the role of the woman that Ouyang Fang was in love with — but he is unable to tell her and she ends up marrying his brother — and Carina Lau played Peach Blossom, the wife of the Blind Swordsman who is separated from him by distance, while Charlie Yeung played a peasant girl possessing only a basket of eggs who is looking for a swordsman to help her avenge her brother's death. In this film all identities and both genders substitute inadequately for each other, with a sense that no single and complete identity can be maintained, certainly no identity that claims to be masculine and complete in itself.

Wong Kar-wai achieved international renown with *Chungking Express* (1994), drawn in plot and inspiration from the Japanese postmodernist writer Murakami Haruki. It starred Brigitte Lin, Takeshi Kaneshiro, Tony Leung Chiu-wai and Faye Wong. The two men play policemen whose troubles lie with their love lives, and who therefore give a feeling of melancholia to the film. The violence is associated with the woman — in this case, Brigitte Lin. The motif of the lovelorn policeman follows *Days of Being Wild* where Tide (Andy Lau) was in love with the first of Yuddy's girlfriends (Maggie Cheung) who does not reciprocate, until, possibly, at the end when it is too late. There is a sequence in which a phone rings in a telephone booth on what used to be Tide's beat, recalling the words of a famous song: 'A telephone that rings, but who's to answer?' Earlier in the film, Tide tells Yuddy's girlfriend to call him, but when the phone rings he has already left behind the police and Hong Kong and gone to sea (he appears in the Philippines section of the film). *Chungking Express*'s less comic successor, *Fallen Angels* (1995), like *Ashes of Time*, was another film about a hired killer (Leon Lai) and his female agent (Michele Reis) who loves him. However, because she has rarely seen him, she has to work out his identity by going through the sacks of rubbish he leaves at his apartment. These lives are crisscrossed by that of the ex-convict, He Zhiwu (Takeshi Kaneshiro), who is falling in love for the first time with Charlie Yeung. Another girlfriend, Baby (Karen Mok), also complicates the killer's arrangements, contributing to his death while he carries out one last shooting. Both of these last two films were set in 1990s Hong Kong, and both tried, through quick cutting and slicing through different narratives, to depict the city's urban space at the point when it could be most mythicized as the story of a successful city whose colonial days, obviously irrelevant to it, were just disappearing. Both films have something of a celebratory feeling within them. *Fallen Angels*, with its characteristic way of contorting images to make faces grotesque and isolating them by shooting with an ultra-wide-angle lens, makes frequent references to *Chungking Express* — most notably with the fast-food restaurant Midnight Express, fast food with a concentration on waste, and rubbish bags.

Happy Together makes a fresh start by not looking back to Wong Kar-wai's previous films. It does not have a double plot. Unlike *Ashes of Time*, it does not have to be seen at least twice before an initial understanding of it can take place. It is pared to the bone with a cast of barely more than three people. Sections of film which were to include the pop star Shirley Kwan were excised from it, so that the film features no women at all. As his second film set wholly outside Hong Kong, *Happy Together* won for Wong Kar-wai the Award for Best Director at the Cannes Film Festival that year, the first time a Hong Kong director received the award. The film was nominated for the Palm d'Or as well. Since *Happy Together*, Wong has continued with *In the Mood for Love* (2000), set in Hong Kong of the 1960s (returning to something of *Days of Being Wild*), which I wish to compare with *Happy Together* at the end of this book.

After *Chungking Express* and *Fallen Angels*, *Happy Together* was perhaps a surprise. Its English title refers to a pop song of the 1960s sung by The Turtles. Its Chinese title (春光乍洩 — Chunguang Zhaxie) is quite different from the English title and awkward to translate. Perhaps 'something sexy's showing,' a cheeky phrase that could be used if a woman inadvertently showed a bit too much when sitting down. Or perhaps the phrase gives the sense of an epiphany or of spring light breaking out. The title has feminine resonances, and in that way it is teasing, given the film's absence of women. It is several things: a Hong Kong film, but one set in Buenos Aires, Argentina, with a closing sequence in Taiwan; a version of a North American 'road movie'; a film about homosexuals and homosexuality made by — for what the statement is worth, and not wishing to be essentialist about categories — a heterosexual director; a film about Hong Kong on the eve of the transfer of power, complete with a televised sequence recording the death of Deng Xiao-ping; a film about exile, or nostalgia, or displacement; and, finally, a film about Hong Kong, or, possibly, about Argentina.

Before thinking about the film as any or all of these things, it will be useful to have an outline of the plot, however bare, to introduce the film to readers who do not know it or for those whose memory is hazy. A fuller account of the film's narrative appears in chapter 5. *Happy Together* depicts the experiences of two Hong Kong men: Ho Po-wing (Leslie Cheung Kwok-wing) and Lai Yiu-fai (Tony Leung Chiu-wai). These two characters' names, as is revealed when the final credits roll, are those of two of the film-crew who worked on *Happy Together* — actually the focus-puller and the gaffer — whose passports appear at the beginning. They are a reminder both of the ordinariness of the names and characters, and of the arbitrariness with which they may be regarded — there is no belief in unique or essential identity subtending this film. The names also imply that the narrative of a Hong Kong team making a film in Buenos Aires replicates a diasporic sense in the film itself. The two men are on the road on the way to see the world-famous Iguazu Falls. Quarrelling, Ho abandons Lai who then finds work in a tango bar in Buenos Aires. Ho later tries to get in touch again with Lai who eventually takes him in again after Ho has been beaten up. Lai responds to Ho's acts of promiscuity by hiding his passport. Lai next begins working in a Chinese restaurant where he meets a Taiwanese man, Chang (Chang Chen), who is travelling the world. Ho ransacks the flat looking for his passport and Lai throws him out. Lai and Chang go to a bar where Lai weeps into Chang's portable stereo. Chang leaves Lai to go to Tierra del Fuego and while there plays the tape recording of Lai weeping that was made at the bar. Lai decides to return to Hong Kong, and works in an abattoir to get more money for the fare. Ho gets in touch again, perhaps to retrieve his passport, but Lai does not see him and leaves for the Iguazu Falls. When Ho arrives at Lai's flat, Lai is in Taipei. Lai goes to find Chang's family's noodle-stall, finding that Chang has left in order to do military service. Lai takes with him a photograph of Chang and boards a train in Taipei, so that the film ends with a sense of that city seen from the train.

The film ends with a sense too that something is about to happen, but refuses to reveal what will actually take place. As the film closes, Hong Kong's hand-over of power from the United Kingdom to China is less than six months away; the future of Lai in relation to his past in Hong Kong or to Chang or to Ho is not discussed; Ho's future is left in the balance.

In what follows, I shall be drawing on a number of texts, films, novels and forms of cultural critique, but it may be the case that none of the people working on the film had any of these examples in mind. For example, the novels by Manuel Puig, which I refer to, may or may not have been read by Wong Kar-wai. But just as the cult that Wong Kar-wai films seem to have encouraged does not concern or interest me, so nor do the assembled materials made available — or about to become so — from rejected parts of the films, which might encourage the view that it is possible to find a 'true' reading of any of the films. Therefore, I have no interest in tracing the director's intentions, declared before or after making a particular film. Biographies or interviews spill out bits of information which turn the film's contexts back into cliché.[2] This is because the 'intentions' are as much unconscious as conscious, and what enables the making of any text or film is a discourse which the author (or *auteur*) cannot be aware of, as it is, or because it is the very enabling condition forming the text's mode of existence. The author is the reader of the text, not the authority to pronounce upon it, and to discuss *Happy Together* requires placing it in contexts which have formed its discursive range — but also finding contexts that will enable us to talk about it.[3] The value of these contexts, both the obvious ones and the new ones which can be found to illuminate the film, is that they cease to be its 'background'. They are illuminated instead by the film which in this way becomes a context for them and enables a further reading of them. The text, therefore, may be said to create its precursors.[4]

2

Happy Together and Allegory

To start thinking about *Happy Together*, I want to look at a term which has been significant in provoking discussion of non-Hollywood film texts and postcolonial writings. I want to do so in order to add into our thinking as many different perspectives on the film as possible.

The American Marxist critic Fredric Jameson caused controversy in 1986 when he discussed Third World literatures — explaining that by 'Third World' he meant countries which had 'suffered the experience of colonialism and imperialism' — and said that 'all Third-World texts are necessarily ... allegorical ... they are to be read as what I will call *national allegories*.' Let us dissect what Jameson says.

He argued — as always in his work — that Western texts were split between showing private and public lives, between 'the domain of sexuality and the unconscious and ... the public world of classes, of the economic, and of secular political power.' In contrast, between this splitting, which repeats a split between Western 'realism' (which shows public life) and 'modernism' (which shows the private sphere), 'Third-World texts, even those which are seemingly privative and invested with a properly libidinal dynamic — necessarily project a political dimension in the form of national allegory: *the story of the private individual destiny is always an allegory of the embattled situation of the public Third-World culture and society.*'[1] The film shows one thing, but it describes another — as happens in allegory. Needless to say, a 'Third World text', for this argument, would include Asian cinema and, specifically, a film such as *Happy Together*.

Jameson's argument has been much attacked, for example, by Aijaz Ahmad who argues against the compulsion implied within his position. Ahmad argues that it would come close to saying that those 'Third-World texts' — which of course, include film, especially if we regard Hollywood cinema as a great neo-colonializing power — which cannot be read as 'national allegories', are by that token not literature, or are not cinematic. If they are not national allegories, then they are excluded from the canon. Ahmad also, of course, argues against the notion of defining the Third World in such a way as Jameson does.[2]

Another critique of Jameson comes from Gayatri Spivak, who takes issue with the idea that there is a single buried or determinate narrative which could be allegorized within the postcolonial text. The unconscious narrative that could be taken from an attempt to give such a thing would rather be one of 'discontinuous interruptions'.[3] (And following also other compelling arguments of Spivak's, I intend to drop the term 'Third World' and use 'postcolonial' instead.) These critiques may be agreed with, but there are still two points within Jameson's argument which can be used when they have been freed from the logic of compulsion which Jameson uses:

1.   There is the relation between sexuality and the public, political

world, which Jameson finds to be asserted within postcolonial writings and film.

2.   There is the idea of the film as allegory.

Both of these points I want to use in discussing *Happy Together*.

Jameson assumes that sexuality goes into the private sphere and politics belongs in the public sphere. This is going over some very familiar ground which assumes that the two 'spheres', one dominated and defined in contemporary thought by Freud and post-Freudians, and the other by Marx and Marxism, are separate and cannot be united. (Some critical theorists, notably Herbert Marcuse in the 1950s and Louis Althusser in the 1960s, have tried to reconcile them.) But perhaps it would be wiser to question the binary opposition between private and public which has been proposed. Could it be that sexuality — including homosexuality — is something constructed by the public sphere? Or what about the other possibility, of thinking that there are not necessarily two spheres at all? For example, that the public creates the private within it? Or that there may be no public sphere, or that it has disappeared? (Is there a public sphere of action in *Happy Together* at all? If so, how is it felt?)

It may be that Jameson's fault is that he has assumed the consistency of these two spheres and also the consistency of the narrative which an allegorical reading uncovers. The study conducted here assumes that *Happy Together* is a much more fissured and divided text than the idea of a 'national allegory' would suggest, and that the narrative does not allow for a division of private and public; of sexuality versus politics. I also think that allegory, in a different sense from that which Jameson proposes, may be a term that is one key for thinking about the film. After all, the film is principally set in Buenos Aires, a city very different from

Hong Kong, yet there is no difficulty in assuming that in some way Wong Kar-wai is always discussing Hong Kong, such as when he shows Taipei in *Happy Together* and his use of Manila in *Days of Being Wild*. That would be following the principle that Marco Polo gives when talking to the Emperor in Italo Calvino's novel, *Invisible Cities*:

> And Polo said: 'Every time I describe a city I am saying something about Venice.'
> 'When I ask you about other cities, I want to hear about them. And about Venice, when I ask you about Venice.'
> 'To distinguish the other cities' qualities, I must speak of a first city that remains implicit. For me it is Venice.'
> 'You should then begin each tale of your travels from the departure, describing Venice as it is, all of it, not omitting anything you remember of it. ...'
> 'Memory's images, once they are fixed in words, are erased,' Polo said. 'Perhaps I am afraid of losing Venice all at once, if I speak of it. Or perhaps, speaking of other cities, I have already lost it, little by little.'[4]

In this way, every city might become, for Wong Kar-wai, a way of describing Hong Kong, an allegory for a city which cannot be shown directly, for, if it could, it might lead to a loss of the subject. The indirectness appears in the choice of images and the mode of presentation of the given city. Therefore, the film is a form of allegory, and although Jameson's division of the two spheres is questionable, it is still relevant to hold on to the pairing of sexuality and politics and to see the film as negotiating these while it questions our assumptions that we know what either of them are. If the film is read as allegory, then both sexuality and politics are also allegorized; both are treated but in ways which do not fit into characteristic ways of thinking about them.

One view of *Happy Together* as allegory ought to be mentioned straight away: that the two lovers stand for China and for Hong Kong, with Taiwan an important other, third presence. The film allegorizes the relationship together of two figures who cannot be happy together, even though they try to start over again. This reading, in my view, hardly takes the film seriously, or the situation of China and Hong Kong. It is, however, the argument of Lisa Odham Stokes and Michael Hoover, authors of the study *City on Fire: Hong Kong Cinema*, though they do not use the word 'allegory', and though, in justice, they do find one or two references to the handover in the film.[5] It can be conceded that the change of power is an issue for the film. But it is also true that the film is not nearly so determinate in what it says or in the way it can be read. Nor does the reading do much for the concept of allegory that has been raised. If allegory means anything, it requires delving into more deeply than this.

Reading Allegory

If the film — a relationship between males — is taken to refer to a relationship between the Mainland and Hong Kong, that means that it can be taken as a representation of something else — that event A in the film means event B outside it. The view of allegory that sees it in terms of what Spivak calls 'discontinuous interruptions' is indebted to two twentieth-century theorists: Walter Benjamin (1892–1940) and Paul de Man (1919–1983). The views of Walter Benjamin appear in his *The Origin of German Tragic Drama* (1926) and they take seventeenth-century Baroque allegory as a way of opposing the Romantics, who downgraded allegory in favour of the symbol. In symbolism, the Romantics believed that the writer or painter found an image which expressed a unity between the thing to be symbolised and the symbol; that the symbol was a part of the object, existed in a continuous relationship with it. The Romantics said that, in contrast, in allegory, the object had *no* relationship with what had to be symbolised: the choice of allegorical image was arbitrary. The Romantics claimed that symbolism was a higher form in that it found a natural (organic) relationship between things. To give two Romantic examples: a red rose could represent a beautiful woman; but what could not be symbolised, because it could not be represented, like Frankenstein's Monster (in Mary Shelley's novel *Frankenstein*, [1819]), was by definition monstrous, unnatural, outside nature which was an organic whole. Walter Benjamin argued that the seventeenth-century writers of 'tragic drama' had played instead on the arbitrariness of the emblems that they used. They had exploited the point that 'in allegory, any person, any object, any relationship can mean absolutely anything else.'[6] This implies two things:

1. That allegory shows a discontinuity between the image (the signifier) and what is meant (the signified), and so it indicates that meaning is always artificial, imposed and not natural
2. That there is no 'natural' way of signifying anything, and no natural mode of representation.

Both points become sharper when we consider the question of homosexuality, which has been classically considered as non-representable (some countries still deny that their nationals could ever commit homosexual acts, which makes them absolutely non-representable within their culture). It remains something monstrous, as unnatural, or to be put of sight. Allegory, as Walter Benjamin uses the term, shows 'nature' to be constructed, so that what is considered to be 'natural' is not that; instead, it is an aspect of ideology that constructs certain forms of behaviour as natural.

Allegory, from the way Walter Benjamin uses it, instead of showing a continuous and steady flow of meaning, fragments that meaning, makes it discontinuous, or interrupts it, and in so doing draws attention to the constructed nature of meanings. When

Jameson discusses Third-World narratives as 'national allegories', he assumes that there is a continuous narrative that can be retrieved from underneath the content of these narratives. But he is not using allegory in the sense derived from Benjamin, because his sense of 'totality', derived from the Marxism of Lukács, wants to argue for a determinate narrative which is concealed as an allegory that can be uncovered. Benjamin's approach to allegory — which is much closer to deconstruction — means that there is not a single buried narrative to be retrieved, only fragments and interrupted moments. Deconstruction, the name given to the critical approach taken by Jacques Derrida (b. 1930), shows that if a text is taken as having a single and consistent meaning, that is because of an investment which has been made in covering over the text's absences, and in creating a single narrative.

Happy Together immediately foils attempts to read it in a single way, such as by its half-replacement of narrative by image, as in all of Wong Kar-wai films. The point about improvisation comes in here. Improvisation cuts across narrative. The film's shots are displaced from context, and, working by themselves, they do not further a narrative — whose nature in itself would be of the most banal. The image comes first, the narrative, usually established by a voice-over, is like an afterthought. The consistency of the narrative is not assisted by the point that more than one voice gives a voice-over, and also not in a way which relates to the other voice. The film works by quick cutting from scene to scene; part of the film in black and white and other parts in colour. Many of the scenes are so darkly lit that the viewer is called upon to create the narrative rather than having it supplied totally by the film's diegesis. The locales in Buenos Aires are barely sketched in; there is no sense of how the characters relate to the city and the shots of the city are increasingly ones of visual overload, where it is hard to read anything definite as they speed by — in the same way as some of the shots of Hong Kong in all Wong Kar-wai's films, from *As Tears*

Go By onwards. Buenos Aires, photographed, especially in the second half of the film, looks like Hong Kong. The ending is as open as anything else in the film, resistant to a meaning in terms of narrative. The voice-overs, of which there are several in the film, are difficult to discuss either in relation to narrative or to a time when they can be imagined as being said. Are they the final thoughts of the characters who speak them, or what was going through their mind at the time? They seem to defy attribution to a specific time and specific place, but this does not take away their authority entirely — I will return to this point later.

These points connect the film to modernist practice, and to the way the city is perceived in film — not as a whole, not even as a series of metonyms (like the Eiffel Tower as a metonymy for Paris, or the Sydney Opera House for Sydney), but disconnectedly, as a series of interruptions. In *Chungking Express* the Hong Kong that is photographed omits any shots which might define Hong Kong for the outside world. (No Hong Kong Bank; no Star Ferry; no Peak Tram.) The same applies to the rendering of Manila in *Days of Being Wild* and Buenos Aires in this instance.

Allegory and Time

Benjamin's view of allegory may be compared with that of Paul de Man's 'The Rhetoric of Temporality', when he too discusses the distinction between allegory and symbol. Like Benjamin, de Man is more interested in allegory, which he sees as different from the symbol since in it, 'time is the originary constitutive category'. The symbol holds together — or such is the idea — the signifier and the signified, which are bound together outside 'temporality'. But in allegory, the allegorical sign only 'refers to another sign which precedes it' in time:

> The meaning constituted by the allegorical sign can then consist only in the *repetition* ... of a previous sign with which it can never coincide, since it is of the essence of this previous sign to be pure anteriority. ... Whereas the symbol postulates the possibility of an identity or identification, allegory designates primarily a distance in relation to its own origin, and, renouncing the nostalgia and the desire to coincide, it establishes its language in the void of this temporal difference. In so doing, it prevents the self from an illusory identification with the non-self, which is now fully, though painfully, recognized as a non-self.[7]

Paul de Man argues that modern allegory is based on this perception of a loss of any origin, which would include therefore the loss of an idea of 'original meaning'. Furthermore, modern writing, modern art and film-making is premised on the perception that we can only say something is like something else when the other has faded from view. The chain of resemblance is, therefore, broken each time. Repetition, which may be the attempt to affirm likeness, fails to do so. Consider how repetition is used in *Happy Together*: it is the binding motif of the film, most consciously so when characters talk about 'starting over [again]'. Repetition makes for recurrent shots such as the Iguazu Falls or the Bar Sur where Lai works. But repetition, far from holding things together, affirms their dissimilarity.

Irony

This point cannot be left without referring to the other term de Man uses when thinking of allegory: irony. Irony is an awareness of the non-coincidence of meaning that occurs when it is seen that signifiers, because they are spatially arranged in a temporal pattern, cannot give anything other than a deceptive appearance of consistency of meaning. Irony means the end of the 'empirical self' which is based on a sense of its self-consistent meaning ('The Rhetoric of Temporality', 216) — so much so that de Man compares it to madness. He writes: 'The ironist invents a form of himself that is "mad" but that does not know its own madness; he then proceeds to reflect on his madness thus objectified' (216). But that does not mean that consciousness of irony is an escape into lucidity. Paul de Man develops this point when he calls irony a 'permanent parabasis' (218), where the last word means 'disruption' — as with an author's intrusion into his or her narrative. This is the source of Spivak's reference to 'continuous interruption'. What is disrupted is the narrative coherence and its systematic quality; it is the mode by which allegory is revealed to be allegory, the putting together of tropes, of figures.[8] But disruption does not bring us back to empirical reality. On the contrary, irony and allegory face the reader, or the viewer, with the constructed nature of the reality that is being seen, and the impossibility of getting beyond that. Irony reveals that we are caught in an allegorical understanding, but to understand at all can only be to understand allegorically.

To summarize how this complex argument and related points by Benjamin and Spivak help in thinking about *Happy Together*, I summarize some points about the film here:

1. The film disrupts our desire to see the characters as representative of Hong Kong or Taiwan, or the events as symbolic of public events;

2. It also disrupts our sense that there is a public narrative to be given of what happens to the characters. We are not able to put together a narrative of the events in Buenos Aires. The voice-overs, which sound like clarifications, are disruptions to a narrative where there is nothing but allegory, and, as de Man hints about irony, such disruptions do not get us out of allegory into reality, but suggest that there is nothing beyond the allegories that characters make for themselves.

3. The absence of Hong Kong from the screen, never seen save

upside-down in Lai's fantasy, echoes the absence of a referent. There is nothing to be said about Hong Kong. This is a Hong Kong film, but Hong Kong is not to be spoken about any more than Buenos Aires is. Neither city is an allegory for the other. Nor does either city define the other by being thought of as opposites.

4. The connections de Man makes among irony and madness and identity are significant for suggesting that the film cannot make statements about being Chinese, or being homosexual, or about the stability of identity itself when that has been transported from one side of the world to another. (The film is 'about' what are sometimes called inverts, as a description for homosexuals. Significantly, the film inverts our sense of Hong Kong by setting it in a place which is an inversion of Hong Kong.)

5. De Man's argument makes the notion of madness a possibility for reading the film. This is reinforced by the point that there is no one outside the events of the film who could give another 'normal' point of view. Perhaps all the characters in the film are homosexual, for instance. (Is that the point behind the absence of women?) The only person who stands outside is Deng Xiaoping, and to adopt and adapt a line from Joseph Conrad's *Heart of Darkness*, 'Mistah Deng — he dead.'

6. The film becomes an allegory of the impossibility of reading, which is itself a theme of the film. People try to read other people's motives, as with Chang's belief that he can hear whether people are happy or not from their voices. (This may be very clever, or it may be a way in which the character convinces himself that he knows things he does not.) Can people's lives be read at all? Lai thinks that he is superior to Ho in that he knows his character, and when he steals the passport — which is, incidentally, the way identity is assigned internationally — it is a sign of that superiority he assumes. But that, of course, may be his mistake.

7. Spivak's sense of 'discontinuous interruptions' as characteristic

of 'postcolonial narratives' fits with homosexuality too, in that homosexuality may be regarded as a disruption of 'normal' senses of sexuality, which are, of course, specially promoted in colonial regimes. Both the sense of Hong Kong as a British colony, or as a city about to come under Chinese influence, and the sense of Hong Kong 'nationalism' — which would feed drives towards post-colonial art — are disrupted by the point that these characters do not fit the way in which sexuality can also be seen as a form of production. Homosexuality might fit with Foucault's definition of madness as the 'absence of work',[9] meaning the absence of production, the absence of producing something usable within a whole economy where nothing is supposed to be outside the homogeneous.

This last point most conflicts with Jameson's sense of 'national allegories'. The concept as Jameson thinks of it cannot recognise the 'absence of work' or the idea that a 'postcolonial' narrative might be a non-productive one. Wong Kar-wai's film disrupts a normal sense of history where it can be said at what point the colonized voice begins to speak. This is not to say that Jameson's terms cannot recognise homosexuality, but I think it would mean that the inscription of homosexuality that he would recognise would demand that it became a part of the national 'work', that it spoke up for individual rights, for instance. It seems to me that the film only very ambiguously can be seen to do this. Which returns us to the question of politics in the film. The 'absence of work' means that the subject occupies a position outside the political as this is consensually defined. (In a later chapter I will discuss the film's treatment of the role of 'work', certainly a prominent topic.)

Later on, we can discuss whether the film actually makes homosexuality integral to itself. It is not, after all, made by a 'gay' director, and the point that one of its actors, Leslie Cheung has a reputation for being 'gay', (whatever that may mean) is insignificant;

Cheung has been associated with Wong Kar-wai in many films.[10] *Happy Together* contains no discussions of homosexuality whatsoever, nor any moments which imply that the film is trying to argue homosexuality as 'natural' or to place it in any context. It makes no attempt to work, therefore, as a 'gay' film. Like the characters who seem to have come from nowhere, insofar as they have lack histories, homosexuality is there but it is not spoken about. There is more than a parallel here with the film's silence about politics regarding Hong Kong and Taiwan. The event of 1997 which the film leads towards, the change of power, is never referred to in the film — for instance, there is no suggestion that the characters are leaving Hong Kong because of their relationship to the changes about to happen.

3

Contexts:
Why Buenos Aires?

That Hong Kong does not appear in *Happy Together* and is not referred to frequently, does not mean that the film is not concerned with Hong Kong or its people. There are some obvious examples, and a few less obvious ones that illustrate the movie's relationship to Hong Kong. The film's language, for instance, is mainly Cantonese and Hong Kong slang. Also, some of the violence between Lai and Ho recalls the situations of *As Tears Go By*. The characters' modes of eating, and their playing of mahjong in a foreign milieu is a reminder of the power of cultural identity. A reference to cinema-going is a reminder of Hong Kong's then near-favourite activity. Perhaps the very absence in the film of mobile phones and pagers, those inevitable markers of Hong Kong society, draw attention to themselves and highlight Hong Kong; like the absence of high technology in this film. But the film also deals with Buenos Aires, and it could be regarded as a tale of two cities, putting them together and almost asking them if they could be happy together.

Buenos Aires, Argentina's capital since 1880, was founded by Spanish colonizers in 1580. To consider this point, we can make some comparisons. Taiwan, where *Happy Together* ends, was settled by the Portuguese in 1590, and Macau, the enclave near Hong Kong which reverted to China in 1999, was leased from China by the Portuguese in 1557. In addition, the Philippines, where *Days of Being Wild* ends, was first reached by the Spanish in 1522, and became a Spanish colony thereafter. Hong Kong, in comparison, was not taken by the British until 1841. Wong Kar-wai's *In the Mood for Love* ends in Cambodia, a French nineteenth-century colony. These colonies, suffering from neo-colonialism — the Philippines from the Americans; Argentina, at the time of writing, from massive demands from the International Monetary Fund (IMF) — may be related to each other. There is nothing accidental in Wong Kar-wai's moving to Argentina after setting the ending of *Days of Being Wild* in the Philippines. The Philippines are represented as a society with no infrastructure, nothing between the really rich (as illustrated by Yuddy's mother living on her estate, cut off from the rest of the Philippines) and the impoverished gangland world in Manila of thugs and prostitutes. Yet the film, while emphasizing these 'Wild West' characteristics, has several shots which unmistakably suggest the old Spanish colonial world. That fascination continues in *Happy Together* which deals with Buenos Aires.[1]

Buenos Aires is also part of an ex-colony. After three centuries of colonial government, Argentina — though not yet called that at the time as it was not considered as a discrete part of Latin America — released itself from Spanish rule in 1816, becoming a federal republic in 1852. Long after its independence, it depended on foreign capital — mainly from the British, who built the railways to carry livestock for export. It became an immigrant society, where 3 million people arrived in the years between 1869 and 1914 — principally men — and found themselves in competition with the existing *criollo* society. (The decimation of a native Indian population was completed at the same time.) Argentina, at a million square miles of territory — roughly the size of India — is the second largest country in South America, second only to Brazil which is larger than Australia. Argentina's areas of pampas for rearing cattle and sheep, provide Buenos Aires with its biggest export manufacture. The beef carcasses that appear in the film recall the city's importance, along with Montevideo on the opposite bank of the La Plata river, to the beef industry. Reference to this industry appears in the film, which picks out, with shots of the abattoir, how Argentina's space may be thought of as dedicated to industrial processes: the manufacture of death and the production of food for a global market. Hong Kong is the opposite of Argentina, at 398 square miles (just over half London's size) with very little land dedicated for agriculture. Buenos Aires's population is double that of Hong Kong. The two places are there for comparing and contrasting. Argentina has often been seen, as in V. S. Naipaul's *The Return of Eva Perón*, as a country which has never been decolonized;[2] but the fate of the nation which *has* been decolonized, is to be reminded constantly that it is a latecomer to the capitalist fiesta.[3]

Latin American literature has been associated with what the Cuban novelist Alejo Carpentier calls 'marvellous realism' (see the preface to his novel *The Kingdom of This World*). 'Marvellous realism' means the sudden appearance of the wonderful, apparently by magic, as though in an epiphany. The Chinese title for *Happy Together* may recall that: Bordwell translates it as 'Spring Brilliance Suddenly Pours Out'.[4] Buenos Aires produced one of the most distinguished twentieth-century writers in Jorge Luis Borges (1899–1986) who in an essay 'The Argentine Writer and Tradition' which incidentally speaks of Argentine qualities of 'reserve, wariness and reticence ... the difficulty we have of confiding, of being intimate,'[5] argued heroically that being Argentinean, out of the loop of Western

Europe and the United States, and similarly distant from Asia, gave one a privilege to take on 'without superstition' and with 'irreverence' the Western tradition.[6] The Argentine writer can read things from this apparently 'marginal' position — this is not Borges's term — that could not be read from the centre. It is the advantage of working from a postcolonial position, to be able to lay hold of other traditions which would be imprisoning to those countries which claim the traditions as theirs. The point, at some level of awareness, holds with *Happy Together*, whose interest in marginality begins with its unaffected awareness of homosexuality — another marginal position which enables perception of what could not be seen from the heterosexual centre.

Part of *Happy Together* may be indirectly influenced by Borges, or by another Argentinean writer Julio Cortazar (1919–1984), whose short story, *Blow-Up,* was used by Antonioni in 1966 for the film of that name.[7] Cortazar's novel *Hopscotch* also could be a possible inspiration for *Happy Together* since it compares life in two cities, Paris and Buenos Aires. But another relevant voice is that of Manuel Puig (1932–1990). When *Happy Together* was filmed on location in Buenos Aires, one of its draft titles was 'The Buenos Aires Affair'. This is the title of a novel by Puig who also wrote *Kiss of the Spider Woman* (1976), filmed by Hector Babenco in 1986. There seems an interesting intertextuality between *The Buenos Aires Affair, Kiss of the Spider Woman* in both its novel and filmic forms, and *Happy Together*. Another Puig novel could be added: *Heartbreak Tango* (1969).[8] This is set in provincial Argentina, though the heroine, Nené, moves to Buenos Aires when she marries — and finds it disappointing. These other novels mentioned are, not coincidentally, set in Buenos Aires (making them city-based). They have a close relationship to the cinema, most evident in the title of Puig's first novel, *Betrayed By Rita Hayworth* (1968), a tribute to one of Hollywood's stars of *film noir*, as for example with *Blood and Sand* (1941). Hayworth made this film with the gay actor

Tyrone Power (the film also plays with motifs of gayness). Puig, who has been said to be gay, was himself deeply influenced by film and had studied film direction at Rome's Cinecittà.

Associating Puig with *Happy Together* suggests three points:

1. The relationship between film and homosexuality; and between both and the city. (*Heartbreak Tango*, set in a small provincial town, makes no mention of homosexuality.)

2. The sense in which Puig and Wong Kar-wai may be making texts about the cinema: *Happy Together* may be seen to be metalingual, a film about film.

3. The relationship between Buenos Aires (the prison, the political situation in Argentina, the power of a heavily masculine society and of men together), and the possibility of relating this to Hong Kong, as this is felt not only in Hong Kong, but by all those expatriated from it.

To develop these points I return to Puig. *Kiss of the Spider Woman* is set in a prison in Buenos Aires, in 1975, when Argentina was under a military government, ostensibly directed by Isabella Perón, widow and third wife of the Colonel Perón who, born in 1899, had been in and out of power in Argentina since 1943, and who had died in 1974.[9] The difference between Perón, as a military ruler and an enthusiast for Hitler, and the military rulers who alternated with him while he was forced out of the country (to Spain, no less Fascist and militarist under Franco), was only a matter of degree. Isabella was to be removed from power by the military junta in 1976: they retained power at least until 1983 (the war with Britain over the Malvinas Islands [the Falklands], in 1982, will be recalled as a late chapter in the junta's history. So will their practice of making dissenters 'disappear' — thus creating the substance of what Luis Puenzo filmed in 1985, *The Official Version*, about the 'disappeared' ones). But probably, in effect the military stayed much longer (and Menim, who became President in 1989, and would have been in power during the period of *Happy Together*, was a Perónist himself. At this writing, one section of Perónists are still in power, and Argentina is in crisis). In the novel, the two men in prison are Molina, (William Hurt in the film) and Valentin (Raúl Julia); one a homosexual and the other a Marxist revolutionary. Though there is plenty of discussion of women in Puig's text, and it would be possible to give a feminist reading of the text, no women actually appear in it, which makes it very similar to *Happy Together*. The novel studies those two topics which Jameson refers to: the sexual and the political. Valentin and Molina critique each other's positions, and both undergo a chiasmic change, whereby Molina becomes politicized, and Valentin, though avowedly heterosexual, and highly patriarchal in his attitudes towards women and homosexuals, engages in a sexual relationship with Molina. But it would be better to say that the text is not 'about' anything so crude as simply a change of character in either men. It is rather a study of identity, which shows that *identity* is formed by *identification* with the other — and here we enter the realm of cinema, which suggests the power of an identification formed by modelling oneself on the other who appears on the cinema screen — an identification which often crosses gender-boundaries. The cinema, after all, may be like Lacan's mirror-stage, where an imaginary identity is conferred on the spectator. Identity, then, is already given, and not inherent; it is received from another, and cannot be seen as fixed. The point about identification with another is discussed by Molina, who spends his time narrating the stories of films where, commonly, he identifies with the heroine.

In contrast to the obviously masculine military running the prison (Buenos Aires is a prison, as Hamlet thought Denmark was), who are patriarchal, reactionary and fascist, *Kiss of the Spider Woman* shows a movement towards something else, which is often coded as feminine. But it is unsafe to work within this binary opposition of masculine/feminine; it is better to say that the 'something else' escapes both terms, as they relate to men and women; it finds something else which may only reductively, be described as homosexuality, since that word implies — as Foucault's analyses in *The History of Sexuality* demonstrate — the fixing of character and the nailing of identity to sexual behaviour. It will be necessary to return to this point. At the moment, it is relevant to turn to Puig's earlier novel, *The Buenos Aires Affair* (1974).

The Buenos Aires Affair was called a 'novela policial' by its author and it reads like a 'hard-boiled' detective thriller, using some of the methods associated with Raymond Chandler: hard-boiled detective thriller films were popular in post 1945 Argentina. Initial difficulties in reading *The Buenos Aires Affair* come from the point that its sixteen chapters weave backwards and forwards in time. Its main characters are Gladys, who models herself on various Hollywood heroines, and Leo Druscovich, and the plot revolves around Leo's need to pretend to commit a crime in order to cover up for another 'crime' which was described in a chapter called 'Leo's Youth', and which has taken place in 1949, twenty years before the pretend crime takes place. With the latter, the novel opens.[10] Leo, aged nineteen, has been propositioned by a man in the street, and his own sexual interest turns into a sadism which ends up in a violent assault on the other man. It is never clear whether or not the man dies, but Leo assumes that he does. Leo has a political interest: he becomes a member of the Communist Party in 1950, but is captured, and under torture, betrays other members. His meeting with the artist Maria Esther Vila, whom he regards as a mother confessor, and her reporting of him to the police (chapter 5), leads to his desire to stage a crime — the murder of a woman — in order that she (Maria) should not think that he might have murdered a man for sexual reasons. He pre-confesses to this imaginary crime in chapter 9. In other words, the non-existent crime is virtually to prevent any suspicion that he might be or have been a homosexual, or might be someone that a homosexual might proposition. It is a defence of machismo: of the masculinity cultivated in Argentina. What Leo does, does not match what he desires — the same is true of Gladys. Both have to cover their actions by fictionalizing. Ironically, Leo is killed in a car-crash, convinced that the police are chasing him in connection with the crime of 1949. This car chase gives, of course, a cinematic ending.

This point about the fantasies the characters live, the very cinema-derived plot against Gladys, and the way Leo pre-justifies it to Maria Esther Vila, is complemented by the way that Gladys lives in an atmosphere of magazine culture and film culture. In an imaginary interview with a reporter from *Elle*, thought up and thought through while she was with Leo, she imagines calling an article on the subject of her romance with the 'glamorously Hitchcockian language "The Buenos Aires Affair"' (p. 100). In other words, she thinks in the terms of the hegemony of Hollywood and United States popular culture, and she is only partially aware of a life outside that of fantasy. In one way, this interest in reality as simulacral is 'postmodern', but it also implies how displaced desires are; subjects in Buenos Aires cannot think through to their desires because these are created elsewhere, which means that Argentina has to be thought of as though it was still a colony, one belonging to the United States. This point can only enrich a reading of *Happy Together*. The government in Buenos Aires — for example the military police department of chapter 5 — is similarly caught up in an atmosphere of newspaper headlines which sideline Argentina for more important 'trouble spots' in an agenda chosen by the US media. In such an atmosphere, which is masculine and fascist, there can be no thinking through of gender-roles or of male or female sexuality; instead, male and female live forms of sexual existence which have been constructed for them.

More corroborative material, both illuminating and illuminated by *Happy Together*, could be derived from Puig's novel translated as *Heartbreak Tango*.[11] This novel, which is about betrayal as is

Happy Together, is a critique of the Argentine hero who tries to exist as a Don Juan. It also shows how the men who live by those standards of masculinity are doomed, and to that end it relies on quotations from songs written to the tango — a dance which appears several times in *Happy Together* (the film could easily have used Puig's novel's title).[12] The first tango perhaps to be written down, at the end of the last century, was the Don Juan tango (it appears in *Heartbreak Tango,* p. 83);[13] but the tango as represented here has lost all its associations with masculinity and become nostalgic, sad, dwelling on the lost past. If machismo society is bad for women, it is not good for men either, whose promiscuity is their only freedom, since they have no economic independence (the point holds for both Ho and Lai in *Happy Together*). They are reduced to a sexual expressiveness, but the Don Juan of the novel dies, like a romantic heroine, of tuberculosis: feminized at the last. His friend, Pancho, having seduced a woman, trains as a policeman (a continuation of the macho theme), probably to get away from her, before he is shot by the woman he deserted. The tango turning melancholic indicates a society consumed by nostalgia for the past, since it cannot face the present, and to people whose feelings can never endorse their desires, what they think they want.

Puig's novels, and the filmed version of *Kiss of the Spider Woman* may have been a direct influence upon Wong Kar-wai. There are points which the texts have in common, beyond the homosexuality and the setting in Buenos Aires, the oppressiveness of that city and the lack of women. There is also the issue of masculinity: that Argentina is identified with 'macho' males who define themselves by a cult of hardness. Naipaul comments on the country's 'machismo' as the conquest and humiliation of women, necessary in 'diminished' men whose lives are in the service of 'colonial mimicry'; this is in the context of watching an Argentine-made film of *Heartbreak Tango*.[14] *Happy Together* does not debase women. Wong Kar-wai has already made fun of machismo in

Chungking Express with Cop 233 and Cop 663 — men in uniform — undoing their authoritarianism, and bringing them into servitude to women (Brigitte Lin and Faye Wong) — as well as bringing masculinity into question in virtually all his work.

It would certainly help to see *Happy Together* as a response to some of the most exciting writing of the twentieth century, and as thoroughly engaged with those Latin American texts. The film has a double context: it looks at two areas of culture at the same time, neither subordinate to the other — for to engage one, the other is also needed. But this does not exhaust the contexts in which *Happy Together* can be seen. Additionally, it is necessary to switch to North America, home of Hollywood's neo-colonizing power, to see a more ironic relationship to an established genre.

4

Contexts:
The Road Movie

Borges' short story 'Rosendo's Tale', set in Buenos Aires, includes a character, Luis Irala, who is embittered because he has been deserted by Casilda — his wife or his girlfriend — who has gone off with another man. He says he is not worried about her, adding, 'A man who thinks five minutes straight about a woman is no man, he's a queer.'[1] The statement may be taken in two ways. Heterosexuality is definable in terms of *not* thinking about women — just using them, which is macho behaviour. Macho behaviour includes a fear of homosexuality, which perhaps, according to the 'queer theorist' Eve Kosofsky Sedgwick, constructs it.[2] One North American version of macho behaviour has been the Western, and another, perhaps a descendant from it, the 'road movie'.

Wong Kar-wai uses Western motifs, especially in his first three films, but *Happy Together* may be considered to be a play on the American 'road movie', teasing the genre, first in the journey to Buenos Aires, and then in the attempts to get to Iguazu Falls. But the suggestion of the 'road movie' is implicit throughout, with

Chang's journeys and Lai's return to Asia from Argentina and the sense that Lai has another journey to make at the end of the film, back to Hong Kong as well as to Taiwan if he wants to see Chang again.

The 'road movie' has been discussed by film critic Timothy Corrigan as a post-1945 genre, and linked by him to a breakdown in the family unit; so that the family's replacement has to be, for the male, the male 'buddy': the brother outside the family. There is a desire, secondly, for technology and speed, which is identified with the truck, car or motorcycle, and a sense that male escapism can take place through technology. Lastly, and most vividly, there is a fascination with masculinity.[3] The key date in the history of the 'road' is Jack Kerouac's novel *On the Road* (1957) which was a memorial to his ten years of travelling, and became the classic text of the 'beat generation' — a term which came into use in 1952, where 'beat' means beaten, upbeat and even beatific. The last meaning, authorizing the sense of some kind of spirituality to be attained through the experience of the road, is, I think, what Wong Kar-wai mocks most in *Happy Together* through the disappointment of the visit to the Iguazu Falls. In the *Washington Post* of 22 October 1969, the year of his death at the age of 47, Kerouac summarized *On the Road* as giving 'true adventure ... featuring an ex-cowhand, and ex-footballer, driving across the continent northwest, midwest and southland, looking for lost fathers, odd jobs, good times and girls, and winding up on the railroad.' The 'road' stands, then, for opposition to mainstream American culture and a new form of democracy and assertion of equality, as well as — the central contradiction — reverence for patriarchy. The narrator, who stands in for Kerouac, goes on the road with Dean Moriarty (Neal Cassady, 1926–68). This character is named for James Dean, and his film *Rebel Without a Cause* (1955), a film which *Days of Being Wild* owes something to for the character of Yuddy as a rebellious youth. (He obviously owes something too to Moriarty, Sherlock Holmes's evil genius.) From the beginning, then, the road genre in novel form received inspiration from cinema.

Later landmarks in the road genre in film included *Bonnie and Clyde* (1967) and *Easy Rider* (1969), but after the 1970s there was a tapering off from making such films despite *Paris Texas* (Wim Wenders, 1984). This reduction has been linked to a growing loss of innocence about masculinity in popular perception, and the sense of the problematic nature of its 'homosociality' — Eve Kosofsky Sedgwick's term to describe a relationship between men, and standing in uneasy relationship to homoeroticism.

Sedgwick argues for the priority of the homosocial bond over any other. For her, it is the characteristic way in which patriarchal society shows itself. The parading of masculinity polices the boundary between it and its other, with which it is easily allied: the homoerotic. The 'return' of the road movie in the 1990s, if it has indeed occurred, with *Thelma and Louise* (1991) and *My Own Private Idaho* (1991) mark a departure from tradition. In Ridley Scott's film, starring Susan Sarandon and Geena Davis, women take to the road and in doing so displace men, and while it is a Hollywood film about women enabling women, it is also capable of supporting a lesbian reading. In Gus Van Sant's film, *My Own Private Idaho*, the road movie is allied with homosexuality and with promiscuity: first seen in the attraction of the narcoleptic Mike (River Phoenix) for Scott (Keanu Reeves). An English film about the road, Michael Winterbottom's *Butterfly Kiss* (1995), showed a service-station assistant (Saskia Reeves) caught up in fascination by a woman on the road with a compulsive lesbian streak (Amanda Plummer) and a desire for her own death by drowning, which she asks Reeves to help her bring about.

Days of Being Wild has aspects in it of a 'road film' when Yuddy goes to the Philippines, followed by one of his girlfriends who is after him. Yuddy is seeking his own death, since he cannot find his mother — or part of his death-wish is looking for his mother. The link between the road movie and a desire for death seems valid, and if this is an undercurrent with the Iguazu Falls moments in *Happy Together*, then that film is in sequence with these films which I have mentioned which imply that the 1990s road movie accepts certain points about the 'road'; that to be on it is already to be marginal, rejecting the politics of home and going outside the boundaries of heterosexual society. (Consider the implications, including the sexual, of the word 'freeway'.) It is as if the film was slyly telling the truth about the road movie as it had once been, the point being that it does not need to emphasise anything about the unconscious of the genre as it showed men together, cutting straight from a male love-scene to showing the two men in the car on the road.

The road movie taps into an aspect of American culture which says that 'our cars and the roads we drive on are one of the few arenas where it is acceptable, and even anodyne, to act out aggression.'[4] Since aggression may be taken to be a key term in Wong Kar-wai's films, and as the sequence in *Happy Together* soon shows the men turning to quarrelling and splitting up, the road movie becomes another mode in which *Happy Together* taps into images and genres which permit violence and displays of masculinity.

But the film similarly advertises its non-American status. The car will not go properly; the technology will not come to the rescue and provide the future that the Americans dream of — the association of the road movie providing the exotic, thus being colonial in its inspiration[5] — and which these Chinese need. The nearest to technology that they have is the lamp of the Iguazu Falls, so frequently appearing in the film, which, like the magic lantern, is the perfect image for the cinematic apparatus: giving the permission to dream and opening up the space for desire.

The road movie may be taken as truly being meta-cinema; film about the nature of film. It is the fantasy of escape which is tourism; of freedom from constraints, which is narcissistic, and of getting to the 'other side of the mountain' — which is what one of the characters in *Ashes of Time* thinks of and speaks about. The film does, after all, show us the Iguazu Falls — twice, in fact. Technology offers the dream to the cinema that the road experience cannot capture. The dream is suffused with nostalgia, for the masculine hero who turns his back on civilization is looking for something purer than what he has left behind, and that purer thing is also a memory, even if it cannot be recalled by the particular subject who is on the road. In that sense, Yuddy's search for his mother is, though frustrated for him, satisfied for the audience who see the mother that he does not. (He walks away down the road, keeping his back turned.) The cinema becomes more satisfying than the experience of the road in giving satisfaction to nostalgia.

It seems as if North American masculinity has within it a nostalgic desire which relates to its sense of being 'beaten'. In the next chapter, which gives a reading of the film, I will compare this reactive masculinity with the tango as an aspect of Argentina and as something integral to *Happy Together*.

5

Reading
the Film

Happy Together opens with a shot of passports being stamped for entry into Argentina in 1995 (so that the action of the film lasts two years), and the two colours of the passports, red for Lai and blue for Ho, dominate the imagery. This scene implies the starting and finishing dates of the action in the *Happy Together*, but since it was filmed using actual passports from members of the film crew as they entered and left Argentina, it is interesting to note that the scene also reveals that the passage of time experienced by the characters in the movie is identical to the time it actually took to film the movie. This fact increases the sense that this film's content comes close to the subject of the process of filming, where a crew must, for instance, be able to be 'happy together' even though they surely would have had their own arguments during filming.

The passport (Hong Kong is a port, as is Buenos Aires, and, in some ways, the men never get beyond being part of a port culture) becomes an element of the plot in *Happy Together*. It is suggestive of cosmopolitanism but also of the idea of a fixed identity. The two colours — which imply over-development (red) and underdevelopment (blue) — undergo several modifications during the course of the film and cannot be taken as indicative of a simple binary opposition between the two males. Red is normally taken as indicative of happiness, or of passion, and in one of its most vivid forms in the film it appears as blood in the abattoir. Blue, a cooler colour, speaks of the sky, or of melancholy (cp. the blues — but feeling 'blue' dates back to the sixteenth century). But, as a romantic character in Manuel Puig's novel *Betrayed by Rita Hayworth* says about Buenos Aires, 'blue and red are, after all, the lights of my city'.[1]

There is another moment of colour in the film when a lamp with the Iguazu Falls painted on it appears and Ho is heard to say 'we could start over' in a voice-over. In this scene, Lai is seen in the mirror wearing blue briefs, and looking disaffected and very unhappy. Next, Lai's narration begins suggesting that this occurrence is in the past. 'Ho Po-wing always says, "Let's start over." And it gets to me every time. We have been together for a while and broken up often. But when he says "starting over", I find myself back with him. We left Hong Kong to start over. We hit the road and reached Argentina.' It sounds as though the film opens at the point of exhaustion. Ho does not have a narrative voice-over, indicating that his experiences are always spoken for, but Chang also gets a voice-over and so enters into the narrative, even if he disappears before the end of the film. Since Ho does not speak for himself, but has a narrative which is given by others, it is not safe for the critic to start criticising him too much, as, in my opinion, Rey Chow does.[2] Actually, very little can be said of him, independent of Lai's perception of his existence as 'happy together' — whatever that means — with Lai.

Lai's voice-over continues as the colour fades away to a black and white or sepia-toned colour scheme, showing the two men on a single bed making love, with Lai on top, with the lovemaking indistinguishable from violence (gripping arms, for instance). It is also very loud love-making: indeed, much of the early film depicts the characters shouting, with Lai, especially, yelling at Ho. Violence, then, takes this and other forms, while Lai's loudness contrasts with his soft-spoken voice-overs.

The love sequence gives way to a 'road' section which is again not in colour. The men are in the car and Lai's voice is heard asking 'Where are the Iguazu Falls?' The two men are going the wrong way to see them. Coming so early on in the film, the road image dominates the movie and gives the sense of a journey never to be completed. At the end of *Happy Together*, Lai will journey to Hong Kong via Taipei, perhaps in order to catch up with Chang, but *not* actually to see him. This gives a sense of being held in a labyrinth — and the labyrinth, of course, has always been the way in which Latin American countries have been seen.[3] The labyrinth is also a challenge to masculinity, which, as in the myth of Theseus and the Minotaur, traps masculinity within it.

The Iguazu Falls in southern Brazil are just above the confluence of the Iguazu and the Parana rivers where the Iguazu forms one of Argentina's borders. (The river, as it flows down, makes a border between Brazil and Paraguay and Paraguay and Argentina as it flows into the estuary formed by La Plata river, on the west bank of which is Buenos Aires.) The Iguazu Falls are a line of waterfalls over 200 feet high, separated by rocky islands, and are wider and higher than the Niagara Falls. In the film, Lai and Ho have been drawn by a souvenir lamp, bought before they saw the Falls (Baudrillard would call this the precession of simulacra), but the Falls also have an existence in cinema, since they featured in Roland Joffé's film *The Mission* (1986) which made them familiar. As the outskirts of Buenos Aires fade in the distance, the car runs into trouble: 'This wreck is useless,' one of them says. When the car gets going again on empty roads the two become lost again, while Lai gives another voice-over explaining how Ho had bought the lamp, that he (Lai) really liked it, and that they had decided to see the Falls before they returned home when they discovered what the lamp referred to. But while they are lost Ho stalks off saying that being with Lai is 'boring' and that he wants to end their relationship, yet 'some day they might start over', to which Lai responds that 'for him [Ho], "starting over" has many meanings'. The last shot of the two men is of them together on road, hoping for a lift back to Buenos Aires. But Ho, who had initially started the relationship, has already ended it. Perhaps ending a relationship, or throwing it away, is part of the process of starting over; to start means also to be able to stop. Starting would mean stopping: that is one of the 'many meanings' that Lai says Ho attributes to the term.[4] The camera interrupts this reflection by showing the Falls in colour, in a shot taken from above (from a helicopter), with both the water and the mist rising from it. At one point, a bird flies over the Falls. As the Falls are shown, in a sequence lasting nearly 90 seconds, the music of Brazilian singer Caetano Veloso performing Tomás Mendez's 'Cucurrucucu Paloma' is played.

Next in the film there is a return to black-and-white photography with a *film noir*-like atmosphere and we find ourselves back with Lai again in Buenos Aires. The city looks like a very European city as the camera picks out its cobbled streets seen in dimly-lit night shots. Again there is a voice-over as Lai explains how he worked at a tango bar, the Bar Sur [South]. People pile in; first a group of Taiwanese tourists, then Ho with one or two others. Ho is smartly dressed in a black and white checked jacket. The sound of the accordion playing the tango leads to a male couple dancing the tango, and then a cut to Ho kissing someone, and then back to the tango and Ho's applause. Lai is disaffected: 'When I came to Argentina, I thought it was big. Seeing Ho Bo-wing again, I didn't want to start over.' The antithesis should be noted: Argentina versus Ho. Space is reduced by the failure of a personal relationship.

The Tango

The tango, which appears at several points in the film, both as part of the soundtrack and as a part of the narrative, has its own colonial history. Like the Habanera, which came from Africa to Cuba (the word is a corruption of Havana), the tango was brought to Argentina and Uruguay from Africa by slaves, and eventually became urban working-class music at the end of the nineteenth century and ballroom music around the time of the First World War. It is tightly written, integrated music, the opposite of jazz's improvisations. As a dance, it is in slow 2/4 time, using, like the Habanera, a syncopated rhythm, and, of course, it requires a couple (back to the film's title) who move at a slow walking pace. Its distinctive feature is '"cutting" or suspending, a break in the motion manipulated by the male or dominant lead skipping a note; obliging his partner to lift and twine her [*sic*] leg round his; he leans her backward from waist up, his hips now against hers in "perfect fit".'[5] Borges has written a *History of the Tango* which argues that its associations with sadness — which fits with *Heartbreak Tango*, and which have been picked up by critics of *Happy Together* — are a decline from its earlier significance. He argues that the tango was brothel music, associated with the new immigrant males and associated with men dancing together 'since the women of the town would not want to take part in such lewd debauchery' and associating it with displays of virility, which, he adds, were carried also in the titles of tango music. The men danced with each other while waiting to take their turn in the brothel. For Borges, the tango showed then that 'a fight can be a celebration'.

This reading of the tango relates straight away to the fights between Lai and Ho — both new immigrants — which open the film, and recur in it sporadically. It also makes the point that the tango, a dance whose use of the body may mark an attempt to free it from colonization, already crosses the line between machismo and homosexuality — it could even be argued that it gave a space for homosexuality. The tango, however, was exported to Paris and came back with its roughness smoothed out. The result is the twentieth-century construction of the tango as nostalgia. For Borges, 'a devilish orgy' became merely 'a way of walking'.[6]

These points about the tango should colour perceptions of the film throughout. Ho goes off with his gay crowd, and the tango continues to play while he looks back towards Lai who is still outside the bar. Then there is silence while Lai is seen washing in the communal bathroom of his apartment-block, and next he is angrily and loudly lashing out at the mirror, in an assertion of masculinity, which is also, because of its negative effect, an expression only of resentment and weakness. The camera returns to the Bar Sur, while, in another cut, Ho is seen undressed, relaxing in a hotel. He returns with his American lover to the Bar Sur. Noticably, Ho is the only one of the two Chinese to speak English as illustrated when he asks for cigarettes and a light. The lighting, purchase, smoking, lack of and sharing of cigarettes is a motif kept up in this film constantly, and possessing several valencies; one connected with the desire to show American 'cool' — applying to both men in different ways — and one illustrating their economic desperation, and one implying their dependence on each other, and still another, seen especially with Ho, smoking alone in the apartment, showing boredom.

Next in the film the inside of Lai's apartment appears, and the lamp, which had been first seen in colour is now seen in the apartment in black and white, becoming a memento, not of the Falls, but of Ho. This part of the movie's action unfolds quickly. It is cold and Lai has a coat on, fitting with some of the very blue-dominated shots of Buenos Aires that run through the film. Colour (yellow and red) appears very briefly with the Cosmos hotel, which is where Ho is staying. He has phoned Lai to come to him. The name fits the rootlessness evoked almost throughout the film —

and the cosmopolitanism on which the film plays, in this, the moment of globalization. The colour recedes when the two men have a fight. Ho wants to make love and Lai, now wearing a black-and white jacket — there seem to be moments in the film when the men swap clothes — is furious and bangs his fists on the walls, a gesture repeated throughout the film, giving another sense of the power of the labyrinth. Lai shouts that he is broke — in contrast to Ho, the kept man — and would have gone home if it had not been for Ho; he had no regrets till he met Ho (this is a statement qualified later in the film). Now his regrets are killing him. Ho says he wants to be with him. Lai storms out, and Ho curls up and weeps, for the first of two times in the film.

The action next shifts to the bar once again. Ho, wearing a dinner-jacket, comes across with a stolen watch to give to Lai so that he can get back to Hong Kong. But seemingly in the next moment, Ho is back in poor clothes and asking for the watch again. (The exchange of the watch seems to be of no more value, and perhaps of less use, than the exchange, or giving of cigarettes.) Lai helps him onto a bus in a wonderfully funny dialogue in which Ho tries to tell him he has been beaten up because of the watch as if he got beaten up in order to prove something to Lai. Being beaten up in a film already full of fighting suggests the continuity of this script with earlier Wong Kar-wai films. It is as if the hoodlums of 1998 in Mongkok, as rendered in *As Tears Go By,* are now in Buenos Aires. Lai leaves Ho, saying 'Don't look for me again,' after giving him a cigarette and lighting it for him in a moment which looks as though it might have been about to turn tender. But then Ho is beaten up again, and arrives at the door of the apartment and collapses. Lai takes him to hospital in a scene rendered predominantly in blue colours. This is the point where Ho, at his moment of greatest physical weakness, says, 'We could start again.' And as the two go home in the taxi in a colour scene, jaunty music is heard playing in the background: 'Tango Apasionata', written in

New York in 1987, and here arranged and played by Astor Piazzolla (1921–1992).[7]

The Yellow Wallpaper

In this scene, the flat is seen for the first time in garish colours, with yellowish-orange to red walls or wallpaper — insofar as it is yellow, we can think of Charlotte Perkins Gilman's *The Yellow Wall-Paper* (1892), a brief record of a woman's madness, brought on further because she is imprisoned by her husband who thinks that rest in this room is the best way in which she can recover. I have already suggested that the film could be seen as a record of madness; a state of neurosis and melancholic anger showing itself in the frequent acts of violence (which understudy the tango), induced by the characters' alienation from everything around them. But yellow is also an urban colour, the colour of a sickness differently expressed by such writers as Dickens, Baudelaire, Dostoyevsky and Bely.[8] The room, seen from various angles, looks cramped and irregularly shaped. It is a room that generates all forms of urban fears, from boredom to paranoia. It is dominated by the lamp and by a single bed, a sofa and a cupboard for keeping cigarettes. The flat has no private kitchen, only a communal one, which perhaps because the lack of privacy has an abnormal, over-exposed, floodlit quality about it. The appearance of the flat at this moment, almost as though it were another character responsible for many of the tensions between the lovers, is marked by the appearance of the sound of music. Ho's arrival at the flat leads to Lai stealing his passport in a mad gesture, perhaps indicating his desire for possession.

The following scene is a shot of downtown Buenos Aires and the obelisk on Plaza de Libertad, on Corrientes and 9 de Julio — an evening shot with traffic speeding by, showing something of the grid formation of the colonial city and giving an alternation in the colour scheme from blue to red. The obelisk is the work of the architect Alberto Prebisch, and was erected in 1936 for no obvious symbolic reason but to celebrate 400 years of the city's existence. The point of the shot is to focus on incongruity, indicating the absurd, presumably phallic, pride of a city that is trying to be Egypt, Paris and Washington all at once. These changes of colour and shifts from colour to black-and-white are signs of what has already been called a continuous 'parabasis' and markers of violent swings in mood, a word whose importance for Wong Kar-wai appears in the title of *In the Mood for Love*, his last film to date. The changes of mood in this film are almost bipolar: from depressed to manic.

The flat, however, which could be seen as an attempt to create a little Hong Kong in Buenos Aires and playing on the concept of home (meaning both where you live and where you come from), does not relate to the image of the public Buenos Aires which has just been offered as a public metonym for the whole cityscape. Outside its range, its existence questions the possibility of seeing the city in this panoramic way. But there is happiness, in a return sequence of the bar, and of Lai photographing Taiwanese tourists, happier now.

In a later scene in the flat, Ho is fed with chopsticks by Lai, his own hands having been bandaged. It is an image of dependency that both men seem to need. Lai wishes for Ho to be dependent on him so that he can be the mother in the relationship. The moment is followed by Lai going down to the corner shop and buying cigarettes — a moment defined by the colour blue. After Lai returns to the flat, there are more beautifully choreographed shots of Ho repeatedly trying to get into bed with Lai, who says to him, with all the dignified suspicion of a heterosexual (as though no sexual preference could ever be lasting), 'Don't fondle me.' And another scene of Lai buying mozzarella — with a flash of Spanish dialogue — for a pizza while Ho tidies up, putting the bed and sofa together whereupon Lai wags his finger at him. But the power-relationships change in the next sequence, where Ho has dragged Lai out jogging in the cold, over a bridge in Buenos Aires where the men are out walking — again blue predominates — and where Lai gets a cold. It leads to one of the most tender and funny scenes in the film where Ho, now back at the flat, asks to be fed and Lai, at his most feminine, is seen cooking and feeding while wrapped in a blanket. A shot follows of Ho's enthusiasm for horseracing — a reminder of Hong Kong's Happy Valley and Shatin racecourses — showing him completely happy, thoroughly energised, as he is in the next sequence of the men being 'happy together'. Here, Ho (in red) teaches Lai (in blue) how to dance the tango in the room. A beautiful shot follows, accompanied by slow tango music, of one of Buenos Aires' poorest *barrios*, La Boca, originally one inhabited by Genoese and other Italian immigrants, and first home to the tango. It appears later, as the name of the destination of a bus. This is the home of Lai and Ho. The shot of La Boca shows the river and shipping to the left, old buildings to the right and an empty street in front. The shot is primarily seen as shades of blues and blacks, with strands of red and white tape in front which have cordoned off an area marked by two oil cans, in yellow and red. This interrupts the tango scene, which then returns when the two men dance the tango in the kitchen, now that the dance has been learned. The two dance and make love in what is surely the warmest scene in the film, with their tender love-making quite the opposite to the violent encounter on the bed at the beginning of the film.

Rimbaud and Verlaine

The street scene, a study in perspective as the street recedes framed by the vertical shapes of the unlit street lamps, is a faint reminder of the road movie. The scene's near emptiness of people and ambiguous lighting, suggesting both dawn and twilight, evokes a feeling of solitude, and, above all, focuses not on the urban or the downtown qualities of area of the Obelisk — an imitation of the Place de la Concorde in Paris — but on its suburban qualities, as a place of rubbish, dreck and forgotten fragments. One analogue for this is found in the poetry of Rimbaud (1854–1891). In 'Ouvriers', one of the prose-poems which makes up *Les Illuminations* — a title which could be compared with the Chinese title for *Happy Together* — the poet describes his exile in London with Paul Verlaine, in 1873, when he was 19. He describes going out one February morning with his partner, whom he calls his wife:

> Nous faisons un tour dans la banlieue. Le temps était couvert, et ce vent de Sud excitait toutes les vilaines odeurs de jardins ravagés et des prés desséchés. ...
>
> La ville, avec sa fumée et ses bruits de métiers, nous suivait très loin dans les chemins. Ô l'autre monde, l'habitation bénie par le ciel, et les ombrages! Le Sud me rappelait les misérables incidents de mon enfance, mes désespoirs d'été, l'horrible quantité de force et de science que le sort a toujours éloignée de moi. Non! nous ne passerons pas l'été dans cet avare pays où nous ne serons jamais que des orphelins fiancés. Je veux que ce bras durci ne traîne plus une *chère image.*
>
> (We were making a tour in the suburb. The day was overcast, and this southern wind excited all the villainous odours of the ravaged gardens and of the dried-out meadows.
>
> The city with its smoke and its noise of factories, followed us far off down the roads. O other world, dwelling-place blessed by the sky and shadows! The South [wind] recalled the miserable incidents of my childhood, my despairs of summer, the horrible quantity of force and of knowledge which Fate has always kept far from me. No! We shall not pass the summer in this miserly country where we shall never be more than betrothed orphans. I wish that this hardened arm does not drag any more, a dear image.) [9]

The *banlieues*, the suburbs, are, literally, the banned places. And that banning appears in Wong's visual image of the cordoned-off street. London in the late nineteenth-century is defined not as the confident imperial centre or as a place for tourism, but as a site of filthy squalor which both renders the space unusable (the dried-out fields) and shadows existence as Rimbaud and his partner, Verlaine, walk out of it. They too are under a ban because, as no more than betrothed child-orphans, their sexual relationship is not recognised by society. *Happy Together* is similarly interested in 'the despairs of summer' and in the way that a gender-relationship becomes one of dependency and infantility, and this shot of Buenos Aires is intense because of it.

The contrast between the shot of the *banlieue* put against the earlier one of the Obelisk, however, also suggests how the city is also banned to the people through a process of Hausmann-like urban renewal which, in the 1930s, tore out the heart of the old city in order to produce the broad Avenida 9 de Julio and the Plaza de Libertad.[10] The Obelisk shot returns later in the film, speeded up, suggesting a more frenetic, hysterical space, made for cars and devoid of people, similar to the shot of the deserted road in the slum. The two evocations of Buenos Aires bear the imprint of a social history of the city which excludes the subject, as figured here in two Chinese gay figures who, nonetheless, are seen doing the tango as if repeating, though in their own way, the narrative of the immigrants who learned the tango at the end of the nineteenth century as a mark of their will to become *portenos* — people of the port city. If the treatment of the suburbs of the city evokes Rimbaud, then the melancholy and sense of exile aroused by the sight of the city made over in the model of Baron Hausmann's treatment of Paris in the 1850s, evokes Baudelaire, in such a poem as 'Le Cygne' (The Swan).[11]

The film next returns to the bar, now seen in colour, where Lai uses a bottle to attack the American who had attacked Ho — a moment of class and political *ressentiment* — followed by a scene in the street near the apartment block where Lai surprises Ho, whom he thinks is out cruising. Lai is again seen in blue (but with a red jacket), as if at these moments of blueness he is most identified with Buenos Aires and with Ho, who wears a yellow jacket, identifying him with the room.

No longer employed in the bar, Lai is now shown at his second job working in the kitchen of a Chinese restaurant. Sound is heard and a voice-over, that of Chang speaking to himself, but not as a narrator, that you can tell it's a restaurant by the sound. The voices speak in Putonghua, so that Cantonese and Putonghua are heard together (and are the respective languages of Lai and Chang). Chang is listening to Lai on the phone, talking to Ho, and thinks that Lai has a pleasant voice. At first, Lai is seen in blue, then in red, and then both men, Lai and Chang, a Taiwanese who has left home and is travelling round the world as a tourist — but has run out of money — and who wants to sort himself out, are in blue. Chang says of himself, 'I wasn't happy, that's why I came' — which echoes Lai's and Ho's reasons for coming. Chang manages to listen in on the phone conversation only to realise that Lai is talking to another man.

Next in the movie there follows a series of snapshots of a relationship composed of images that do not connect narratively. Ho searching the flat, jealous over the idea that Lai may have another lover; Lai equally jealous; scrapping and fighting; Ho asking Lai whether Chang likes him, followed by another moment of jealousy when Lai tells him to get out. These fragments, which are humorous as both characters try to retain dignity and a sense of the self in impossible conditions, are followed by another series of more tender scenes first showing Lai working, apparently doing mending-work on a roof. Ho comes up to him, and nuzzles him and tries to bite him while below, by the water's edge, young people play, followed by a shot of the sky. Next, a brief moment in the restaurant is shown, and then the ghostly sense that Ho has gone from the flat. At this moment, the furniture in the flat is seen in a blue light. Then Ho returns with food, saying that he had gone out walking because he was bored. Next, Lai in another sequence comes back with cigarettes — to stop Ho from going out at night. These are followed by a football sequence, where the men who work in the restaurant are relaxing outside in a backyard — a little heterotopic but enclosed space — by kicking a ball. The colouring in the football sequence is a deep blue and full of shadows. In this scene, Lai comes in and disrupts the game and walks off as Chang looks on. It is one of those scenes which reinforces Chang's sense that Lai is not happy. The feeling is that Lai's return to the room is to find Ho going out; his promiscuity taking him over again.

Football

This is the second of the film's references to football (the first was Ho listening to a radio commentary in Spanish), a same-sex activity which is a reminder of one of Argentina's most representative activities and, like the tango, one appropriated by Argentina from its 'colonial' beginnings — it was introduced to Argentina by the British around 1867. It is an index of masculinity. Its skills are not unrelated to the tango, either. The body's feints in both activities are essential as is the legwork, so that the equivalent in football of the intricacies of the tango is the dribble. Diego Maradona, Argentina's most notable football player and through whom Argentina won the World Cup in 1986, was born in 1960 in one of the poorest parts of Buenos Aires and rose to international stardom as the most skilled dribbler in the game.[12] The football scene is set against another of Argentinian music and of people in the restaurant playing mahjong while Chang looks on. In a black-and-white toned scene, the Lai's voiceover continues with him saying, 'Some things

I never told Po-wing. I didn't want him to recover too fast. Those days were our happiest together.' His words are a reading of events which qualifiy the sense of what has been seen, and make it clear that no single narrative can be given for what is being seen and that there is no obvious definition of 'happiness'. But this moment, which signals Ho's new strength and a shift in his power-relationships, is followed by a colour sequence which reverses the pattern set earlier in the film — whereby colour seems to go with the warm or the glamorous moment — with Lai, in a fit of depression, banging at the wall with a knife and sitting despairingly.

The film returns to the kitchen of the apartment where a woman is briefly seen, something that is in striking contrast with what has been dominant in the film so far. It is followed by the incidents surrounding the passport which Ho has had taken from Lai, and shows examples of Lai's possessiveness. A heavy blue toned exterior shot appears of the bridge where earlier on the men had had their disastrous jog, and then the film cuts from this to scenes in the flat. Rimbaud may be evoked again, in his poem, 'Les Ponts' (The Bridges):

> Des ciels gris de cristal. Un bizarre dessin de ponts, ceux-ci droits, ceux-là bombés, d'autres descendant en obliquant en angles surs les premiers, et ces figures se renouvelant dans les autres circuits éclairés du canal, mais tous tellement longs et légers que les rives, chargées de dômes, s'abaissent et s'amoindrissent. Quelques-uns de ces ponts sont encore chargés de masures. D'autres soutiennent des mâts, des signaux, de frêles parapets. Des accords mineurs se croisent, et filent; des cordes montent des berges. On distingue une veste rouge ...
>
> (Skies crystal-grey. A bizarre design of bridge, here straight, there curved, others descending obliquely at angles to the first, and these figures renewing themselves in other circuits of the lighted canal, but each so long and light that the banks, weighed down with domes, abase themselves and shrink. Some of the

bridges are still loaded with hovels. Others carry masts, signals, fragile parapets. Thin wires cross and fade; ropes mount up from canal banks. You can distinguish a red coat ...)[13]

Here, in this sequence of disconnected imagistic sentences which highlight their lack of connection and in doing so bring into question whether bridges actually bridge, there are still those bridges which, amongst all this visual excess — which is also there in the film — bear signs, carry signals, or suggest meaning as forms of bridging. The bridge in the film reaches back in time, and fits, too, the lack of connection which is also an odd connectedness between Lai and Ho. The exterior sequence is followed by a view of the apartment and then Lai's loneliness is focussed in a slow, two-minute sequence which shows him on a boat going around the harbour in Buenos Aires on the Rio de la Plata, the estuary formed by the meeting of the Parana and Uruguay rivers. The scene is intensely blue, and accompanied by music. There seem at least two valencies to this moment. Firstly, it is not the Iguazu Falls, being, instead, flat and surrounded by signs of industrialism, such as the shipping. Secondly, it is not the harbour in Hong Kong, place of the largest port in the world and the antithesis of this dreamy, ghost-like sequence. The camera focuses on the wake of the boat that Lai is in; dwelling on the after effects of his having been in Buenos Aires.

Chang

The film moves back to the kitchen, seen now with its tiles as yellow, and with the implication of drinking taking place there. The scene continues on back to the room where during the night Ho leaves as if for good, leaving Lai in bed. It is the second clearly defined time when Ho has walked away from Lai. It establishes a pattern of repetition. Ho no longer feels he needs Lai; yet, in going without his passport, it means that he will come back and that the two are in a necessary relationship which cannot finish however much one may walk out of the door. Every *fort*! (gone) will be followed by a *da*! (here).[14] To walk out, after all, is to walk further into the labyrinth. The action reverts to the football, and then again to the kitchen, signalled first by a huge tureen of red soup, and to Chang being asked to go to the cinema by a Chinese woman whom he refuses — this scene is virtually the only moment when a woman is seen or heard. 'I don't like the girl's voice' he says — on account of it being, he says, too high. Chang declares that he only likes deep and low voices in women. The comment invites speculation and shows that Chang is particularly identified with voices, with the erotics of the voice and with hearing. Chang's interest is in what can be deduced from the voice and its timbre. It is another eroticism which is at work here, less obviously focussed on the body and more on sound. There is the sense that there might be a growing attachment between Lai and Chang, for having turned down the woman, Chang asks Lai if he wishes to go to a nightclub later.

The club they go to is called the Three Amigos (friends — both the number of them, and the notion of them are significant in view of the title), and the dominant colour of the scene is red. Chang and Lai are drinking, and Chang is again listening so that he is able to detect that another group of men are about to fight, which he can hear in the tone — or mood — of their voices (rather than by listening to what they say, which is incomprehensible to him because it is in Spanish). The men *do* promptly get up to fight, as though living out Chang's idea of then. The brawl is, apart from a scrap in playing football, the first time that men other than Ho and Lai have been seen fighting. Chang says that when he was a boy he had eye problems, which made him a good listener, and adds that 'I think ears are more important than eyes. You can see better with your ears.' And 'you can pretend to be happy, but your voice can't lie. You can see everything by listening.' Perhaps in contrast to seeing the other person, which may imply intimacy, the ability to hear them stresses the possibility of love or a relationship at a distance. It is not necessary to see someone in order to hear them because voices carry. This is the moment when Chang intuits that Lai is not happy. Film, supposed to be a visual medium, installs in it the need not just for synaesthesia, but also the sense that it depends on the voice and on sound.

The scene moves on to football set in the summer and Chang's voice heard in a voiceover. Music is then heard and the action shifts back to the Three Amigos and to Chang announcing that he is leaving — just as the summer is ending. He is going to the lighthouse at the end of the world (too cold a place for Lai to go to). Lai says that he has heard that at this lighthouse people can dump their emotional problems. Chang gives Lai a portable stereo-recorder and tells him to speak into it so that the recorder can carry away his troubles. This is once again a moment which comments on the possibilities of film, escaping trauma, through film's ability to remove suffering by articulating it. When Chang is off-screen in the club, Lai holds the stereo and cries into it. This is Lai's only moment of weeping, which is framed by Ho's two moments. One is left to wonder for what Lai is weeping. For Ho? For the impending loss of Chang?

A moment of farewell between Lai and Chang follows, one of the most tender moments in the film such as Lai and Ho's tango-dancing, and a moment that holds the action. Chang calls Lai the blind hero, the Blind Swordsman of Chinese legend, thus returning to the notion of the superiority of the aural over the visual. The Blind Swordsman is also a reference to *Ashes of Time*. A long embrace between the two follows. It is succeeded by a voiceover from Lai in which he says that he could feel Chang's heart beat, another suggestion of the shift from what is visual to another form of sensation and something that certainly raises questions about the desire in both men.

Sleepless in Buenos Aires

The disappearance of Chang is followed by another shot of football, but this time of professional football played by Argentine teams — the location was the stadium of the Boca Juniors, called La Bombonera[15] — and then a speeded up night-shot of Buenos Aires showing the city in its most alienated form. These city shots which follow are accompanied by music and, for the first time, by English voices singing about being happy together. ('Me, happy with you, you, happy with me' — an expression of pure narcissism, of lovers as a mirror to each other.) The irony is set against Lai, now at his most alienated, who sees Ho in a public lavatory — here the shots are all dominated by blue — with the implications that both men are promiscuous and similar to each other. Lai, only less romantic, says in a voiceover that he thought he was different from Ho but now realizing that all lonely people are the same. That sense is increased by the next scene which shows Lai sitting in a cinema, where gay love-making is taking place on the screen, and making sexual contact with a white man next to him. This scene prompts in the voiceover which follows a narrative about the reasons for his leaving Hong Kong in the first place, which are now revealed to have nothing to do with his relationship with Ho. The mood is confessional and it goes along with the spirit of the tango which also provokes confession:

> My obsession, heartbreak tango
> plunged my soul to deepest sin,
> as the music of that tango
> set my poor heart all a-spin.[16]

It relates to Lai saying that he now feels no different from Ho. He has stolen money from one of his father's business partners and his boss; he has wrecked his relationship with his father. The stealing compares with Ho's theft of the watch. Both men have been enticed into trying to move into a different class and they have both manipulated men (a form of tangoing) in order to do so, with predictable results. Lai's reflection on his father leads to him picking up the receiver of a blue-coloured public telephone in order to ring him — but his father does not respond when he rings — and to sending a Christmas card, which turns into a long letter. The motif of starting over again reappears as he says, 'At home I didn't talk to him. Now I want to tell him many things. I don't know what he'll think after the letter. In the end I say I hope he'd give me a chance to start over.' In this sense of the importance of the father — the significance given to the patriarch will be recognised in such a film as Ann Hui's *Summer Snow* (1995) — there is no reference made to the mother.

The desire to leave Buenos Aires and to return to Hong Kong, suggested since the beginning of the film, leads Lai to work in an abattoir. The 'Happy Together' music reappears. It is his third job in the film and, as if he were descending into Dante's Inferno, the least representable of the forms of work he must do. He has gone from being doorman at the bar (public) to the restaurant-kitchen (not seen by the public) to the abattoir (what must not be seen). His jobs compare with Ho's, who, as a rent-boy is also the unrepresentable part of urban life. Yet, as Lai becomes more unrepresentable in Buenos Aires, working by night, he gets nearer to Hong Kong because, with the twelve-hour time difference from Hong Kong where everything is reversed, to work at night is to work when Hong Kong people are working by day. The same pattern is at work in Dante: the bottom of the Inferno is also the ascent to Purgatorio. It is also a moment when Ho tries to phone Lai again because he wants his passport back. When Lai wonders how Hong Kong looks upside down, upside-down shots of Hong Kong appear — Causeway Bay, Kwun Tong, and East Kowloon, with a soft soundtrack of Hong Kong voices and the signature tune for the news, that agent of globalization which links everywhere to everywhere else. The upside-down shot works like the tango. The first time the tango was seen, the man leading turned his partner upside down at the last. The reversal of time that takes place in inverting Hong Kong, which has its analogue in so many Latin American narratives which dispute the primacy of linear time (Borges, Marquez, Cortazar, Puig), has its other analogue in the tango.

The Iguazu Falls

Scenes of the abattoir return: The men are seen showering after working with the bloody animals and a moment when Lai is hosing down the blood — which the red now signifies — after he has been seen showering. A moment occurs when Ho knocks on Lai's door, though Lai is asleep under a blanket as red as the blood; but then Ho leaves. The camera stares down two corridors as if emphasising the labyrinth. On his way out of Buenos Aires, Lai leaves Ho's passport on the table in the apartment and hires a car to see the Iguazu Falls before going. The tango music returns and there are shots in colour of the road. Lai is seen through the car windscreen driving and drinking from a brandy-flask, another moment which establishes him as in an American road movie, and him as self-possessed, in charge of himself. Yet he is opting to see the Falls without Ho. Indeed, it is impossible for him to do so *with* Ho and the shot of him through the windscreen, sitting alone, emphasises the loss; what we see gives expression to the Lacanian meaning of castration, as the inevitable condition of the desiring but disempowered subject.

There is a further cut to Ho at the Bar Sur, wearing his yellow jacket, and dancing a tango as if in a dream, or as if an automaton, with the male dancer who danced for the tourists at the bar. But as they turn, the shot is of Ho dancing with Lai again. The scene is followed by silence and a shot of the street outside the bar where the birds are singing as if to suggest this is the dawn of another day. Ho is next seen slumped on the pavement. His watch moves from 23.59 to 00.00, perhaps marking the change from 1996 to 1997, but it is not certain. It could be any day and any time, for time as measured digitally seems to lack a context, to be simply the automatic passing of minute by minute measured by an endless round of numbers unrelated to circumstances. Earlier in the film amongst the city-images there had been a shot of a more monumental clock with four faces giving a sense of time as having a universal address but, nonetheless, looking anachronistic now, existing only a for a moment.

There follows a shot of Ho in the apartment putting out the cigarettes, cleaning the flat up, fixing the lamp of the Iguazu Falls so that it shines in colour again and then sitting on the bed and howling. That is juxtaposed with Lai reaching the Iguazu Falls and saying, 'I finally reached Iguazu. Suddenly I think of Ho Po-wing. I feel very sad. I believe there should be two of us standing here.' The rotating shot of the Falls from above that was seen much earlier reappears, and the view is held longer while the music which plays is the 'Tango Apasionado'. The Falls are seen, in a sequence which lasts for two minutes, as water disappearing into a vast hole, a vast gap. It gives an image of absence and also implies that the end of narrative he has desired by making this journey is a form of death. He has come thus far and has completed a quest, which means that he has reached a point of stasis — no more deferral, no more delays — so that that position is truly one of death. It is only because he is still not happy that he can continue. The narrative cannot reach the totalizing power of the final metaphor which would complete it.

It is January 1997 and the voiceover of Chang is heard as he arrives at his lighthouse at Ushuaia. This town, the capital of Tierro

Fuego province which is part of the Tierra Fuego archipelago, is divided in sovereignty between Argentina and Chile and separated from the mainland by the Strait of Magellan. It is part of Argentina, and the most southerly town in the world at the southernmost tip of the Americas. Chang can not go any further. The locale adds to the sense of *distance* which the film gives (and it contrasts to the northern direction in which Lai has gone). It focuses, too, its interest in *borders* which begins with the passports and concludes when Lai reflects that Chang has a home to return to: a home being that which has secure borders. Borders take other forms, such as those between people and people's bodies, and which are focussed in the anxieties Lai has about sharing or not sharing a bed with Ho. Borders raise the question how people can be 'happy together', and borders are disturbed by such a game as football which depends on going over and transgressing the other's border; they are violated by sound which does not respect borders and which Chang is sensitive to: hearing across other people's borders.

Taipei

Chang says that he could not hear anything on the tape that Lai had given him save what sounded like sobbing. Perhaps in the location, there is an echo of Virginia Woolf's modernist novel *To the Lighthouse* (1928), where going to the lighthouse opens up many possible significances, none, however, possessing a single symbolic value. The action shifts to the Three Amigos, where Chang has come back, en route for flying home, to find Lai. As the day dawns there is the sense of night-time in Taipei. A symmetry with Buenos Aires's daytime appears as Chang wonders if the night market in Taipei is beginning yet. A sequence follows of a Beijing television reporter announcing the death of Deng Xiaoping. It is a tale of four cities: Buenos Aires, which is now left behind, but which still contains Ho; Beijing and Taipei, where Lai has arrived, and Hong Kong which has not yet been reached. This film about 'deviants' makes a final deviation from Hong Kong to Taipei. Lai says, giving a voiceover from his hotel, that he arrived on 20 February 1997, the day after Deng's death. At the moment of return from Buenos Aires the presence of technology becomes more visible, as if bringing out a lack of synchronicity between time and experience in Argentina and those concepts on the other side of the world.

Lai looks for Chang in the night market, finding the stall where Chang's family works selling noodles and tofu, identifying it by the photos of Chang, one of which he steals. Another voiceover is heard, as Lai reflects that this is the place where Chang, on military service, can always return. 'I can see why he can afford running around so freely. There's a place where he can always return. I don't know when I'll see him again; what I know is, if I want to, I know where I can find him.' Saying that he will return the next day to Hong Kong, he boards the MRT train in night-time Taipei (the mass transit system in Taipei, in imitation of Hong Kong, had just opened). Speeded up, this goes round above street level on a bridge whose carrying power cannot be doubted. Bordwell says Lai is 'carried by a night-time Taipei train into a cataract of speed and light'[17] and coming to rest at a station, a perfect image for the film's non-closure. The roofing can be seen overhead but ahead the track is receding into the background. The music of Danny Chung follows: 'Happy Together' — 'I can see you and me being happy together for the rest of my life.'

The music sounds upbeat but it also depends on an hysteria which is visible in the speeded-up conditions in which people in Taipei are seen, which also relates to the dominance of technology in the city. The same speeding-up appeared in downtown Buenos Aires, as a marker of alienation, perhaps distinguishing the downtown from the suburbs. Here, alienation is all-pervasive: the train encompasses Taipei, and it means that the energy which the night market signifies has become hysterical, theatrical, obsessive, like the music. Notably, too, the yelling that took place earlier in the film is heard again in the cries in the night market. Nothing is repressed within the city, but that absence of repression may be a desire to repeat out of a desperate anxiety to affirm what cannot be affirmed.

The film showed two hotels and ends not in Hong Kong, but in a city whose relationship to its powerful neighbour, mainland China, is as embattled as Argentina's relationship to the USA. That point should not ignore differences however, as Taiwan, though it may have no representation in the United Nations and has an ambiguous political status altogether — which makes discussion of it as 'home' ironic — has also been presented as a place with an economic power Argentina lacks, for Taiwan has been exporting coach-loads of tourists to Buenos Aires. The film responds to the power of globalization, but it may also be seen as 'minor' since all its points of reference are contestatory of 'real' places of power: there is no New York or representation of the United States, and no China either. Beijing is flattened out to a single representation on camera. These forms of world power, or empire, are missing. Taiwan, Buenos Aires and Argentina and Brazil are presented deliberately as alternative bodies of power. The absence of Hong Kong from these representations means that it exists in 1997 as either and neither of these two sides of a binary opposite, just as, in the alignment of Taiwan and Argentina, it is not clear whether Taiwan is the same or different from Argentina.

6

Happy Together and Homosexuality

It was, perhaps, surprising that a Hong Kong film should be so open on the subject of homosexuality. Though homosexuality was part of the plot of Yip Wai-sun and Kwok Wai-chung's *Mongkok Story* (1996)[1] and had appeared before, for instance in Peter Chan's popular *He's a Woman, She's a Man* (1994) (a Leslie Cheung film also starring Anita Yuen, about genders being confused by characters in disguise),[2] homosexuality was only de-criminalized by the British colonial government in 1993. Chan's film was asking for tolerance and recognition of homosexuality. The cool temperature of *Happy Together* can be gauged when it is compared with a more popular Hollywood-inspired film, Ang Lee's *Wedding Banquet* (1993). This film, which showed a gay Taiwanese (Wai-tung, played by Winston Chao) in middle-class New York working in real-estate — of all bourgeois occupations — and in a relationship with an ultra-professional type — a doctor (Mitchell Lichtenstein) — broke no taboos. It may be suspected that it was made for Western consumption by someone who knew that a 'screwball' comedy about gay people would play well, and it implied that Taiwanese morals and Taiwanese patriarchy could make the adjustment to Western standards which, of course, it accepted as normative. It is worth recalling, too, that *Wedding Banquet* intended to have the allegorical feel about it that some people have looked for in *Happy Together*. The gay couple, happy together, are Taiwanese and American; the woman (May Chin) they try to help — Wai-tung's tenant — is Shanghainese and in need of a Green Card; so Taiwan and the Mainland can also be come together. There is the suggestion too that Taiwan has entered the modern world in its ability to accept homosexuality. In contrast, *Happy Together* makes no attempt to 'Westernise' homosexuality by making it thoroughly bourgeois and linking it to a secure income and a stable relationship. *Wedding Banquet* allied homosexuality to body-building and other such practices which not so silently 'redeem' homosexuality by making it the purest form of masculinity.[3] That the healthiest male, able to dispense medical advice to all, is gay, and a doctor, is another attempt to sanitize the homosexuality. The characters in *Happy Together* are working-class and though they are good-looking enough for the screen, their income would bar them from a fitness-centre. Their homosexuality stands independent of any such prosthetic, and when they are sick, it is not sentimentalized. Whereas *Wedding Banquet* included a fetishizing of the male body, it is part of the politics of *Happy Together* that nothing like that occurs there. Furthermore, *Wedding Banquet* implied that each homosexual was a caring and sharing figure ready for fatherhood and for a warm, if relatively non-sexual relationship with a woman. That was part of its Hollywood character. Lastly, *Wedding Banquet* flaunted its allegiance to a certain Chineseness which could be defined in terms of keeping up traditions. *Happy Together* has no such sentimentality about being Chinese.

Contrasting *Wedding Banquet* and *Happy Together* — neither made by 'gay-identified' directors — means recalling that as with everything else, every inscription of homosexuality is both a *representation* of it and a *production* of it, including a production of knowledge about it. These terms bring us onto ground discussed by Michel Foucault in *The History of Sexuality* and applied by Edward Said in *Orientalism*. Said's subject is how the East, the Orient, was created by Western imaginations and by Western colonialism, which claimed the privilege of being able to describe and to account for what it had created. Said was working with Foucault's model which argued that sexuality had been brought into heightened representation in the nineteenth century, and coded in relation to different character-types who were thereby produced as subjects. Foucault argues that the concept of the 'homosexual' comes from the late nineteenth-century, 1869 being the time of the word's first citation. The homosexual as a character-type is produced in nineteenth century discourse, and does not appear in previous literature, though homosexual acts may have been made the subject of that literature's discourse. It is not that there 'is' such an entity as the homosexual, rather, the character-type comes into being when homosexual acts are seen as produced from a character whose instincts are homosexual. The act comes from an actor, a person who must confess to being a homosexual.[4]

It follows from this that every text which shows a 'homosexual' adds to the production of the homosexual; it is not neutral. The presentation of the homosexual in *Wedding Banquet* is as bourgeois, capitalist, masculine and tender-hearted, just as he is all-American. Such an image, which of course subordinates Taiwan to Hollywood's neo-colonialism, obscures other possibilities of representation such as, for example, those in Jennie Livingston's documentary film about black and Hispanic gays in New York's Harlem and Brooklyn, *Paris is Burning* (1990). This film, which showed men in drag, with almost no money, attempting to camp up a life of high fashion as women, gives another representation. This is not to say that *Paris is Burning* is 'better' — and 'documentary' should not be taken as conferring objectivity on the film, which was much criticised as being an outsider's: a woman commenting on men's same-sex desires.[5] Rather, every version of homosexuality contains a production of the homosexual as an essential type, which makes it inherently oppressive in Foucault's terms, since what is produced, with whatever 'good' motives, is fictional, a product of discourse, where the homosexual action engenders the reification of a recognisable type, an entity called 'the homosexual'. And every representation articulates with what can be represented — with what is representable. As stated before in chapter 2, some things in any particular configuration remain outside representation, outside the discursive limits — the ideology — that allows some things to be said and others not.

Before leaving *Paris is Burning*, it may be added that the film has been influential in 'queer theory'. I have referred to this through Eve Kosofsky Sedgwick (chapter 4). Other theorists are Judith Butler, Michael Moon, David Miller and Diana Fuss who have argued for the priority of being 'queer' — a word reclaimed from being a term of contempt — over being 'straight'. Queer theory could make little of *Wedding Banquet* because that film assimilates homosexuality to American norms, making Chinese customs odd, or risible, perhaps as a way of laughing Americans out of their national homophobia. Queer theory derives from Foucault, and emphasises that there is no essential homosexual nature. It suggests that 'normality' involves repression in that it holds that heterosexual desire is 'natural', and not constructed. If all forms of sexuality, homosexual and heterosexual, both plural, not unitary forms, could be seen as constructed, discursive and not as the products of natural choices, this would be a liberation which would show that 'gender' itself — the division of people into male and female — was also a discursive category. *Paris is Burning*, in that it shows men wishing to be women, is obviously 'queer' in showing that homosexuality causes 'gender trouble'.

Critical Issues: Sexuality in *Happy Together*

Considering the arguments of Foucault that a film about homosexuality produces a particular form of knowledge, and those of Said which question whether any group can be represented by another, especially by a more powerful majority, it will be seen that a number of controversies surround *Happy Together* and its subject matter.

One argument runs that the film is not about homosexuality at all; that it is just about relationships, which happen to be homosexual, but could just as easily be heterosexual. This would make the film an allegory, in the accepted sense of that term — though we have seen reasons why A cannot be described in terms of B, and that there can be no movement from describing one form of sexual partnership to describing another. Nonetheless, the view received a little support from Wong Kar-wai who said, 'It's not a gay film. It's a love story about being lonely with somebody else; being happy together could also mean being happy with yourself, with your past.'[6]

Another view holds that the film is affirmative about homosexuality by actually representing it, not bothering to discuss it and certainly not justifying it, treating it as no different from any other sexual partnership. A more negative reading argues that the subject is not portrayed from the inside, but from an outside position; that the director-and-writer and the camera-crew are presenting a topic they know nothing about, speaking for it from a position which describes and constructs it (the arguments follow Edward Said's ideas). As men cannot speak for women, so some feminists argue (and can men be feminists?), can 'straight' people speak for homosexuality?

It should be noted, too, that the film works from the standpoint of Lai, played by a 'straight' actor, Tony Leung; while the 'gay-identified' actor, Leslie Cheung, plays a role that is more irresponsible and immature. The voiceover, camera positions and narrative continually reinforce the point of view of the 'straight' actor. Some critiques suggested that Leung never convincingly represented homosexuality, even in those scenes which required him to act the promiscuous gay. The film's narrative adds to the marginalization of the other: Ho ends the film as a solitary man, whereas there is some future indicated for Lai; there is the sense that he has been freed from his trauma. Lai's destiny has to do with reconciliation with his father, which implies a movement back towards the centre.

The absence of women from the film is implicated in the representation of homosexuality. Is it 'essentialist' to say that this means an absence of the feminine? How does the absence relate to homosexuality? It cannot be accidental, but does it imply that, even if women are not spoken of negatively, that homosexuality is misogynistic and deficient in not relating to women? What is to be made of the point that Lai relates, apparently, only to his father?

The first argument — that the film could just as easily be about a man and woman — relates also to the question of the film and the feminine. Excluding women could be seen as a marginalization, but that argument would be stronger if the men in the film were empowered by their absence. They are not, because they are not empowered at all. They have virtually no social contacts at all. Their lives are studies in *anomie*, as colonized subjects in an alien city. The absence of women is their deprivation, though it is not commented on as such, and it puts them in the position of having to be women themselves, something seen most in the moments when Lai is cooking and feeding Ho (moments reminiscent of *Kiss of the Spider Woman* in both its versions, when Molina nurses the sick Valentine). Or the moment expands what is meant by 'masculinity' by changing the definition.

Lai's actions with regard to Ho contrast with the caring male's attitudes in *Wedding Banquet*. There, the argument runs that homosexuality has made the men more appreciative of other people. This is part of the film's 'feel-good' character and its comic genre. Here in *Happy Together*, there is simply less articulation of any position. Lai cooks for Ho for a number of reasons which include warmth of feeling but also economic necessity. (This film is 'about' work and work conditions.) Time and again with this film that is the point: the class positions in the film, which barely need open referencing, oppose Hollywood middle-class standards. Masculinity and femininity relate to class as categories; gender cannot be isolated from economics.

It does not seem interesting to see the film as allegorical of heterosexual relationships, even if it were possible to allegorize in that way. It leaves out the film's specificity, and the way it opts for the marginal. It *could*, however, be argued that the film is about men learning to be women. This might relate to arguments from Jacques Lacan about sexual difference being set up through language. Lacan argues that a subject-position which is assumed by entry into the symbolic order always opens up desire. To examine this requires a reminder of some of the key terms of Lacan, and of their critique by Jacques Derrida. The 'symbolic order' is governed by language. Entry into it as into the sphere of culture,[7] as different from the child's primary attachment to the mother, takes place under the auspices of patriarchy which compels access to the mother to be routed through language, not in the tactile bodily way assumed before that, in the child's dyadic relationship with the mother. Language delays and defers access to the mother, and, as a structure of difference, it impels on the child the learning of sexual difference. To take up a position within the symbolic order as either male or female implies a loss of what Freud considered was an earlier bisexuality.[8]

The male's positioning within the symbolic order brings it into direct competition with the father — indirectly alluded to in *Happy Together*. The boy must give up the mother as the focus of desire, which instils another loss, and is a source of melancholia concentrated on the lost object. Entry into language is also entry into single meaning ('what exactly do you mean?' is the demand placed upon the growing boy) — because of the dream of language meaning one thing and not another. The father seems to govern the power of language to possess a clear referent; Lacan refers to the 'paternal metaphor' or the 'name of the father' where the notion of phallic power seems, ideologically, to guarantee the stability of the signifier in relation to the signified.[9] The dream of meaning in language being one thing and not another, not dual or plural, makes the feminine that which does not conform to single meaning, but which is double, poetic, de-stabilizing.

Derrida's arguments draw out the plurality, or the difference within language; he accuses Lacan's psychoanalysis of being complicit with this, referring to Lacan's work as phallocentric, or 'phallogocentric', having the belief in language being on the side of clear utterance, and of a deliverable message.[10] In Derrida, the feminine is the difference which returns to haunt language, and sexual choice itself, in so far as phallocentrism implies that learning sexual difference within language imposes sexuality and sexual preference.[11] Homosexuality becomes a moment of contestation whereby the symbolic order misnames the subject, and opens it up to desire. Indeed, no sexual choice can satisfy desire, since the binary distinction male/female, part of the structure of the symbolic order, cannot answer to the bisexuality of the being not coded within the symbolic order. It follows that no one can be outside the state of desire; this applies both to heterosexual and homosexual choice. Desire is played on in the film's English title, and in Ho's wish to 'start over' again. When Lai drives towards the Falls, he looks happy and integrated — he is moving towards a place of desire. When he reaches the Falls and is not happy, it is a crystallizing moment when he knows he can either be with Ho and not at the Falls or he can be at the Falls and not with Ho, and neither state would produce happiness, the fulfilment of desire. The gap that desire opens up makes sense of the emphases on distance noted in chapters 4 and 5, and it also makes sense of Lai's relationship with Chang which again only works by distance. Ho, and, to a lesser extent, Lai, are both promiscuous, which, on one reading, relates to an argument made by Freud that 'something in the nature of the sexual instinct itself is unfavourable to the realization of complete satisfaction'. Freud contends that 'the final object of the sexual instinct is never any longer the original object but only a surrogate for it. Psychoanalysis has shown us that when the original object of a wishful impulse is lost as a result of repression, it is frequently represented by an endless series of substitute objects none of which, however, brings full satisfaction.'[12] I take away from this, not the argument that the mother is the original love-choice, barred in the Oedipal stages, nor the question whether sexuality is an instinct, and in what sense, but the words 'surrogate' and 'substitute' which make all sexual choices metonymies for each other, in an endless displacement which refuses finality and makes for the onward continuation of narrative. There is also the point that the partner and the desire never converge. A sexual partner can only be a substitute for something else. The most striking example of the substitutional is the Iguazu Falls, which Lai sees without Ho. Lai's situation throughout is no different from Ho's, for he is halfway between Ho and Chang. Unable to be happy with Ho, there is no guarantee that he could be happy with Chang, whose happiness he desires because he feels he lacks it — but this is not tested, because Chang has also said that he was not happy. Appropriately, when Lai comes to Taiwan to find Chang, he is not there, which means that the nature of his desire, and whether it ever could be satisfied, cannot be tested. Learning to be women, as referred to earlier, then, would mean not men giving way to an ideological view of women as carers and learning to behave as such (this the men do already, anyway), but rather learning to accept the otherness of desire, and the double nature of any subject position; the recognition that no gender positioning can be stable because of the doubleness of inscription within the symbolic order.

This argument helps with the question whether the film is negative about homosexuality. It is possible to agree that it is, but not because homosexuality is represented from the outside. Lacan's demonstration of the repressed plurality implied in any subject position, the impossibility of the single-subject position, invalidates the notion of a heterosexual or homosexual identity. Nobody can speak from inside a subject-position since all such positions are states of desire. They do not represent where a subject is, but where the subject would like to be. To claim to be able to speak because one is a woman, or a gay, or Chinese or a postcolonial subject is an essentialist position. Each of those subject-positions stand ready to be contested by someone making a purer claim to being a woman, or gay, or more Chinese, or more oppressed by the colonial system. To announce a pure position is a denial of difference that would disallow the claim of someone within a group to speak for the group.

But in *Happy Together* no one makes any identity claim at all and the most interesting relationship is between two men who make no avowal of an identity to each other at all — Lai and Chang. Whether Chang has any sexual interest in Lai, whom he sees as the older man, cannot be articulated for the reason that Chang seems to have escaped the necessity of defining himself in straight/ gay terms at all. Foucault argues that 'western man has become a confessing animal'[13] by which he means that the constraint is on the modern western subject to demonstrate his/her subjection to the power of the discourse of sexuality by acknowledging himself or herself to be just the character-type that the discourse pronounces them to be. Chang has no sense of the need to confess, though interestingly he has the listening ear that might mark him as a confessor (the person who hears a confession). It seems that he admits to no character, no single identity, as regards to sexuality. Rey Chow misses that point when she complains that Chang's character remains 'largely undeveloped';[14] in saying that, she is, unconsciously, arguing for a further production of the subject.

The drift of these arguments imply that it does not help to ask whether an actor who is not gay-identified (such as Tony Leung) can adequately 'represent' a homosexual. We cannot work within a critical paradigm where it is asked if the actor is sufficiently realistic in a part, because that assumes that the audience already knows what a particular identity looks like — which is to accept the power of ideology and the received idea. The movement of *Happy Together* is away from an exhausted mode, where definitions have been given, and going slowly towards something else, where at least two out of the three characters can start over again. Its drift is towards the future, which outpaces all possibility of definition, indicating that to speak of character-types only fits past models which it cannot be interested in. The model that asks an actor to represent a type we think we know assumes an essentialist and non-constructed nature of reality. The film is not realist in working from an assumed empirical model — one of the reasons why its setting is Buenos Aires, place of defamiliarization, where any form of behaviour for the film's audience is likely to be slightly awry. In discussing it as an allegory, it is more relevant to think that its actions point to something which cannot be said to exist, rather than to anything knowable. Homosexuality itself may be allegorical, pointing towards ways of rethinking gender which are as yet inchoate and have no actual place.

7

Happy Together, Hong Kong and Melancholy

Happiness

There are many comic moments in *Happy Together* which reinforce the sense that the characters do enjoy happiness together as well as suggest that happiness may also not necessarily be recognised as such, but may be the product of adversity and difficulty. Yet in narrative terms, the presentation of Lai and Ho's lives together is negative. The title of the film is complex. It could be read as two interrogatives i.e. Happy? Together? This could make the two halves of the English title constitute an oxymoron (that is, a statement where words of opposing meaning are brought side by side), so that the question is this: Is happiness possible when people are together? Is happiness a joint or a shared thing, or does it depend on isolation or solitude?

The song's words, 'I could be happy together with you', add to the ambiguity, for 'together' could be part of being 'with you' or it could be part of 'happy' — as in: I could be 'happy together' with you, meaning I would be 'together', I would be happy with myself. So I could be 'together' if I was with you; which might also include the meaning that I could be 'happy together', and yet without you. Being 'happy together' and being with the other person might not be wholly related to each other. The concept of being alone, in rugged solitude belongs to a particular inscription of masculinity within American popular culture — it is celebrated, for instance, in those road novels and movies whose theme is isolation, getting away from other people and whose lesson is that happiness can be found only in separation. But this, which implies that you can be happy (together) *or* together with someone, also qualifies the idea of happiness, for happiness which is outside a community requires a special definition of the term, and a denial of togetherness implies that 'happiness' should be seen as an absolute, as an unqualified possession, outside any difference which would come about from interaction with another.

The title, then, could be seen as a study in contradiction. Happiness which was not also together would not be happiness. Happiness which depends on being together, however, informs the concept of happiness with something other to it. That is, happiness ceases to be an absolute quality. Happiness which is outside the concept of the other, and the other's difference, by trying to be an absolute (as with the American masculine hero, whose pride is that he is alone) must fail, as must all single, unmixed qualities.

Further, when the other is another male, definitions of the concept of '*homo*sexuality' need to be called into question. The root of 'homo' is a Latin word meaning 'the same' — as in homogeneous. ('Homosocial' may be an unhelpful neologism, in assuming that 'homo' comes from a Latin word for 'male' or 'man'.) The 'hetero' in 'heterosexual' comes from a Greek word meaning 'other'. Hence the word 'heterogeneous'. The word 'homosexual' is ideological since it contains the implication that in it there is no relationship to the other — where the other, in male homosexuality, would be the woman. The words 'happy together' make problematic a relation with otherness. Does 'together' mean that happiness can only come from a togetherness which denies otherness, alterity? Does the title mock the notion of a relationship to the other, since no 'other' — no woman, and no male who is not Chinese — plays a significant role in the film?

But that could be contested by the argument that Lai and Ho are the other of each other. It could be argued that the pressure of what the poet and critic Adrienne Rich calls 'compulsory heterosexuality'[1] makes the construction of *hetero*sexuality a relation to the same, to the homogeneous — a relationship in which the person never steps outside of line. Homosexuality would then, oddly, be a relation to the other since it steps outside the realms of homogeneity. Homosexuality could be a form of heterosexuality — a relation to the other — and heterosexuality a relation to the same, a form of homosexuality. That is an argument from 'queer theory'. But there is no need to invert the terms heterosexuality and homosexuality. Heterosexuality may or may not be a relationship with the other; homosexuality, despite its name, which prejudges, may or may not be a relation with the other. The other certainly cannot be defined biologically, as 'the opposite sex'.

It seems that here is one of the anxieties that construct *Happy Together*. The fear implied in putting a word like 'happy' at the front is that the film may be about unhappiness. Happiness, as discussed already, may be already delegitimated as a concept, depending on the status or lack of status to be given to the word 'together'. The threat overtaking any relationship is that its togetherness may involve an occlusion of otherness; that it may be a relationship with the same. In which case, at the centre of the film there would be no difference, but rather *in*difference, a term whose implications ramify. Indifference to the other person is particularly what is feared in this film. Lai ends by walking out on Ho, which may be a form of indifference to him — or may be the best thing for Ho or for them both. A homosexual relationship particularly challenges by raising fears of indifference, since ideologically it carries the stigma of eliding sexual difference. Perhaps the fears of indifference are what motivate the promiscuity the film shows (this also has an economic basis). The homosexual relationship becomes inscribed with a particular fear of indifference, which is melancholia. The more overtly 'masculine' love-making of the opening of the film is reactive, a response to a sense of emotional failure which, like a piece of syncopated music, starts the film off. While *Happy Together* never critiques homosexuality, it is aware of different forms that it can take, some of which are more protective of masculinity than others, where 'masculinity', as in the tango or the road movie, may be a reactive formation, a desire to protect the self from the fear of emotional failure, or indifference in relation to the other or a fear of the other's indifference.

Sexuality and melancholia pair with each other, as do sexuality and politics. The film is 'adult' enough not to patronize homosexuality by suggesting that it is necessarily positive. Unlike a film which might come from a gay-identified director, it does not feel that it needs to be affirmative on the subject. It can, rather, think of it in negative terms because those are produced by the politics of Hong Kong and of Buenos Aires alike. This returns to Jameson's point about the two spheres of sexuality and politics but it also inverts it. Sexuality and politics are determined by each other, in fact they *are* each other. No politics can exist outside the sexual, and no sexuality outside the political. It is an arresting moment when Lai tries to ring his father and gets no response across the distances. Is not that silence inseparable from Hong Kong's politics? Silence from the patriarch compares with the even deeper silence which comes about with the death of Deng Xiaoping, another figure of patriarchy with whom desire and fulfilment show themselves not to exist in a punctual relationship. Deng was, famously, waiting for the moment when he could tread on Hong

Kong soil, when it would not be the property of the colonizer, and would not visit Hong Kong before June 30, 1997. It was his version of reaching the Iguazu Falls.

The father's silence raises the question posed in chapter 6 about Lai's relationship to patriarchy. It is not that the ignoring of the mother points to a sexism within the film, rather that the subject can get no validation from the past or from the figure who, for Lai, embodies Hong Kong values. Is it to be assumed that the father has no tolerance towards homosexuality, or that he cannot accept someone leaving Hong Kong? Is it, following Chang's point, that he will not, as it were, give himself away by speaking since the voice tells so much about unhappiness and is therefore what reveals personal vulnerability, or a failure of masculinity? Whatever the reason, it is clear that it is the father who has the problem, not the son. Perhaps if the first reason is valid, the father's problems are related to homosexual desire himself. That was the subject of the Taiwanese film, Tsai Ming-liang's *The River* (1996).

Lack of validation from Hong Kong, or from China — or even from Taiwan, which, after all, made Chang unhappy — links to a sense that in the film patriarchy undoes itself. Both these points articulate with the sense of the characters being in a place (Buenos Aires) with whose history they can have nothing to do. That point would construct nostalgia. The Argentinian essayist and novelist Ernesto Sábato has seen the two principal attributes of the immigrants to the Argentine since 1900 as being 'resentment and sadness'.[2] Marta E. Savigliano quotes Sábato:

> It was not [sex] that the lonely man of Buenos Aires was worried about; nor what his nostalgic and even frequently cruel songs evoked. It was precisely the contrary: nostalgia for love and communion, the longing for a woman, and not the presence of an instrument of his lust. 'In my life I had many, many *minas*, but never a woman.' [This is a tango lyric: Mina, incidentally, is

the wife in Puig's *Betrayed By Rita Hayworth*.] Tango expresses an erotic resentment and a tortuous manifestation of the inferiority complex of the Argentino [this is a reminder of postcolonialism] since sex is one of the primary shapes of power. Machismo is a very peculiar phenomenon of the *porteños*. ... The porteño feels obliged to behave as a male to the second or third power ... The guy carefully observes his behavior in front of others and he feels judged and potentially ridiculed by his male peers.[3]

The same point may apply to the immigrants in *Happy Together*, who, though Chinese, replay the history of European immigrants of the beginning of the twentieth-century. The tango, as cleaned up by Paris, with its 1920s mournfulness over failed romance, its existence as 'a sad thought set to dance rhythm',[4] makes it clear that masculinity becomes a reaction to failure, the failure of experience. It constructs the subject as melancholic, and exiled from a distant land, where he could find love — hence nostalgic.

Nostalgia

The road movie, the tango as discussed and as remembered in *Heartbreak Tango*, the cult of masculinity and of solitude and the labyrinth — each of them points that have been discussed thus far — are all productive of nostalgia and seem to suit Rey Chow's assessment of the film. To these points may be added Lai's references to 'home', at the beginning of the film when he remarks that they wanted to go to the Iguazu Falls and then home, as well as his comments on Chang having a home. They also fit a nostalgia-motif, though the first reference is made more complex by the point not yet acknowledged that Lai cannot go home because of his relationship with his father; home can be only a wish for Lai. Other Wong Kar-wai films may be read similarly: Yuddy's desire for his mother and the Blind Swordsman in *Ashes of Time* who wishes to see peach blossom once more (this being the name of his wife as well).

Rey Chow thinks the film is nostalgic towards Hong Kong and she makes the claim that it is subtended by a desire towards a primal — she calls it primeval — union which she thinks the film most openly gestures towards in the vision of the Iguazu Falls. She writes: 'In the tumescent form of the waterfall, image has now become All, exuding an overpowering feeling of oneness that seemingly transcends the interminable, volatile human narratives around it.'[5] Criticising Lai's desire to imagine an upside-down Hong Kong as 'infantile', she thinks that the screen, in turning Hong Kong upside down, acts like a 'magic wand', making something come true because it has been fantasized.[6]

I think this reading needs probing. Taking the second point first, the upside-down shot of Hong Kong does not appear so much for Lai's benefit, but to further defamiliarize the audience, most of whom — for those of whom Cantonese is their first language — are seated the right way up in Hong Kong itself. The sequence invites Hong Kong audiences to turn Hong Kong upside down themselves, which would mean to read the film in a carnival manner. And an inverted Hong Kong is only that: it is a literalization of what Lai has said, and so it mocks the desire by asking the person who wants to see Hong Kong upside down what she really wants. And to take the Falls as such an image of 'unmediated presence' requires forgetting that they are seen twice, and that when they appear for the time when they subjected to this reading, that is a repetition of something seen before. The reading also ignores the soundtrack, which playing the tango, even though this tails off, asserts doubleness — the image is not one thing, but visual and aural together. Repetition can never allow for unmediated presence, because repetition always entails difference, and is a reminder that the first time an image appears is never enough to establish its being. It depends on the second occurrence which hollows out the first appearance, and has no continuity with it. Above all, the repeated image — repeated also in the music — presupposes the possibility of yet another iteration, which would be another in a series, but still without the ability to establish the meaning that was lacking the first time. This is to return to de Man's arguments in 'The Rhetoric of Temporality' on allegory; and it implies rather that the sight of the Falls, which the first time Lai does not see at all, and the second time when what he sees cannot be the view that appears on the screen (a product of aerial photography) exists as a form of indifference. Earlier, I characterized the second view as death, as the disappearance of desire into a black hole. If the Falls *did* represent the achievement of meaning, the final patriarchal metaphor, that would indeed be death, because it would be the end of narrative based on the deferrals and repetitions of metonymic desire. But it has no such finality, as Lai's voice-over makes clear. Lai is still sad, the Falls exist as an image of indifference, the failure of desire. The Falls make him wet, as if casting something of this influence upon him. Such indifference is also implicit in showing Hong Kong upside down. What difference does it make? It is the 'same' Hong Kong only turned round by a trick of the camera.

If Rey Chow finds nostalgia in this film, as she does elsewhere in Hong Kong cinema, in a related way David Bordwell finds in it sentimentality and a lack of irony, since he argues that Wong Kar-wai's films, 'like classic rock and roll, take seriously all the crushes, the posturing, and the stubborn capriciousness of young angst. They rejoice in manic expenditures of energy.' He relates Wong Kar-wai to Truffaut, as opposed to Godard with whom Wong Kar-wai has also been compared, for instance by critics in *Sight and Sound*, for his use of 'not quite grown-up characters brooding on eternally missed chances'. Earlier, he has said that 'Wong has yet to make a film organized around an older person's fantasies', the youthful people in them 'are often living out childish fantasies'.[7]

The critique is problematic in using French cinema by which to place Hong Kong cinema. Perhaps irony in the non- de Man sense is an achievement of a society at the point of exhaustion, commenting on its own development and power to shape the development of others, in which case it is a difficult model for Hong Kong to follow. Irony in this sense is problematic in that it assumes a controlling narrative which is wiser and more disillusioned than the characters in the film. The ironist is above the situation and speaks from an assured standpoint. Certainly *Happy Together* is not like that, but the argument that there is no irony neglects the question: Where can the text speak from? Where can a Hong Kong film take its judgments from? From the colonial power? From the Mainland? What form of history has it had which would enable it to situate judgments except from those of another discourse equally not its own? In going over to Latin America the film shows its sense of the problem and that may be the form of irony that the film works with. But Argentina, poised ambiguously between different forms of colonial rule and haunted by the United States perhaps allows no more here than Hong Kong does. The danger in the critique is that the comment on 'young romance' risks becoming a comment on Hong Kong itself.

The lack of irony Bordwell detects in Wong Kar-wai generally should be related to *Happy Together*. Yet it is hard to think of a scene in the film which cannot be read doubly; even the ending, which some people read affirmatively. A film which so much plays on repetition is certainly aware of the duality that is possible to read into all situations, even the most intense and perhaps apparently fulfilling. Rather than Truffaut as the analogue for the film, it might be worth shifting the argument to Rimbaud, where personal bitterness, which links with sexual transgressiveness, is inflected by political anger — as it is not in Truffaut — and the emptiness of the city as described in *Les Illuminations* relates to a failure of politics. Like Rimbaud, the gay lovers of *Happy Together* make little effort to appropriate the city as, say, characters in a Dickens novel do — they do not make Buenos Aires their own domain. Their only way of relating to the city, indeed, is through promiscuity, that most impersonal and indifferent, if intimate, relation to the other in the city, but which stands in no opposition to romantic love. Actually, promiscuity is necessary to such love, as is seen when Lai and Ho, at their most dependent on each other, try to outdo each other in citing the number of lovers they have had. At such a moment, where love seems dependent on the other having had many lovers, however much this may be negated, an irony enters in which gives yet another meaning to the phrase 'happy together'. Promiscuity, as an opposite to paranoia, might be seen as the mode which city existence encourages; and it would certainly fit with the fragmented images of the city which appear at this point. They run by fast at the moment when Lai, free from Ho and with Chang gone, is alone in the city. The fragmented and momentary shots, whose being cannot quite be determined, that is, it cannot be said precisely what they are images of, relate to the anonymous and temporary sexual partners that the two men find. Cinema becomes a mode to display promiscuity, insofar as both relate to the city.

Bordwell's critique is of adolescence and narcissism — these qualities most on display in *As Tears Go By* in the character of Yuddy. The terms need further analysis, and one way might be to remember that the key term for discussing Latin America has been the word 'solitude'. I refer to the Mexican writer Octavio Paz (1914–1998), in his book of essays on Mexico, *The Labyrinth of Solitude* (1950). Paz, defining 'solitude' as a predominant quality in Mexicans has been followed, or anticipated, by other writers, including Borges and in the Columbian writer Gabriel García Marquez's novel *One Hundred Years of Solitude* (1967) and in Puig. All have seen it as a problem throughout Latin America. Paz writes that 'Narcissus, the solitary, is the very image of the adolescent.'[8] He means that

Mexico is not yet adult; hence it is not yet equipped for the modern world.

Now this argument about solitude links with other points discussed in this study. For example, the solitude wished for in the road movie, which infuses it with nostalgia; the celebration of masculinity as a lonesome state and the relationship between solitude and the labyrinth, which has already been related to the road movie, but which could be borne out in other ways such as by considering the shots of corridors moving away from Lai's apartment, or, earlier in the film, Lai's running away from the hotel where Ho is staying in a speeded-up moment where the angles of the walls and street are all oblique. These examples may be of adolescent states, and it should be added both that the road movie is narcissistic in tendency, and Lai appears that when he is seen through the windscreen (in film, so often an analogue to the mirror), driving by himself to the Falls.

Nonetheless, Paz's formulation points the way to see something unsatisfactory about Bordwell's conclusions. One point about *Happy Together* is that, with certain qualifications, there is an absence of narcissism throughout the film, including in the love relationships, that is made obvious when Lai smashes the mirror. There is some narcissism in seen in Ho's character, such as in the scenes where he has successfully joined with a gay crowd, but it does not last. As always in this film, the failure of narcissism is linked to economic failure; the people here do not have the money to possess the necessary attitude required for narcissism. Sentimentality and narcissism and solitude all are linked in that they all require self-possession, belief in the integrated ego, or subject.

If nostalgia is an aspect of sentimentality, the point applies there too. Sentimentality may seem to be like melancholia, but in fact the two qualities may be deduced to be opposites on a line of reasoning made by Freud. He distinguishes mourning from melancholia on just the basis of the relation each affective state has to subjectivity: 'In mourning it is the world which has become poor and empty; in melancholia, it is the ego itself.'⁹ That latter state describes Lai when Chang tries to analyse him as unhappy; but it should be added that the sense of impoverishment for these migrants from Hong Kong is already pervasive, and part of this film's politics, so that when Lai confesses in a voice-over that he has stolen from a friend of his father's in Hong Kong — a subject which would be the basis of such a film as *As Tears Go By*, which is all about petty thefts and inter-family strifes — that is part of the regret that he has been carrying round with him throughout the film, a regret which has also impoverished him and made him feel worthless.

Films such as Wong Kar-wai's, which so obviously put nostalgia at the centre, or discuss it, are not by that token nostalgic. Nostalgia, expressed within so many of the co-ordinates which make up this film and make it implicitly generically nostalgic, runs against the quality of excess in the film which prevents the nostalgia-genre expressing itself in single terms. But also, it becomes apparent that nostalgia is the dominant ideology which is almost inescapable and which therefore necessarily appears in the film. It is what constructs the subject. As part of the 'cultural logic of late capitalism',¹⁰ nostalgia is how the past and memories of the past are made a fetish within Western modernity. But that does not mean that the film can be taken to conform to its cultural surrounds.

Melancholia

Nostalgia depends upon a prior belief in the integrity of the self, so that there would be a conviction that if the self were to travel back to its homeland, it would feel at home there or it would be able to relate to its past. The film is more ironic about, for instance, the convergence of Lai and Chang upon Taiwan and Hong Kong at the end as a desire which is repeated in the film. To concentrate on that 'homecoming' means forgetting the character of Ho and also to assume that those traumas which the film has shown can be overcome — for instance, to think that Chang is not simply giving way to a tourist's sentiments when he thinks that unhappiness can be left at the end of the world. Melancholia splits the relationship between the subject and its past. The fragmented form of the film negates the possibility of reading the subject in a single way, and presents as an alternative to the nostalgic subject the melancholic one — who, for reasons in addition to those already discussed, which have to do with homosexuality — has the sense of its own being as ruined.

For Ackbar Abbas, in Wong Kar-wai's films 'the image always subtly misses its mark. It misses its appointment with meaning, and turns into that characteristic Wong Kar-wai thing, the image of disappointment.' He relates the boredom that is a subject of the film (Ho thinks Lai boring when they are travelling to the Falls) with a melancholia that he finds relates to an experience of *space*, as boredom bears on the experience of *time*.[11] Time and space, however, cannot be so separated. When Ho says he is bored, which indeed implies that there is nothing else other to be experienced than what Walter Benjamin calls 'homogeneous, empty time'[12] — a term which brings the two concepts together — he walks away from the car, which is one form of space which has no inherent relationship to either of the men, as well as being barely functional, into empty space. Gesturally what he does is also empty and, accordingly, the camera cuts to another moment when the two men are seen in a long shot, in the middle distance, held in time and held in space as they wait by the side of the road, which stretches both before and behind them and in both directions. But it makes emptiness and the threat of that a powerful element within the film.

Lai and Ho come to Argentina, a place defined by huge spaces, in contrast to Hong Kong, in order to 'start over'. It is as if Buenos Aires is a photographic 'blow up' of Hong Kong. One danger of space is that discussed by the surrealist Roger Caillois — for part of his life an inhabitant of Buenos Aires — who discusses a fear of identity-loss suffered by schizophrenics. 'They answer the question, "Where are you" by the answer, *"I know where I am but I do not feel as though I'm at the spot where I find myself."* To these dispossessed souls, space seems to be a devouring force. Space consumes them, digests them in a gigantic phagocytosis. It ends by replacing them.'[13] In the film *My Own Private Idaho*, discussed in chapter 4, the 'answer' to this fear is narcolepsy: 'a kind of hysteria in that it is a reaction to intense psychological and emotional tensions'.[14] As a modern fear, this assumes that there is something twentieth-century about schizophrenia, a position which has been tentatively argued for by Louis Sass, who aligns it, as a particular form of madness, with modernist practice. But it should be possible to go further than that in the case of *Happy Together*, where none of the subjects is shown at home. As economic migrants as much as anything else, with a separation from 'home' the meaning of which intensifies for Lai as he goes on, they are dispossessed, exiled. Their territory is nowhere. For Lai it moves from the outside of the bar, to the furthest inside of the restaurant; or places which are under ban — the public toilet, the abattoir. If fear of spaces is a dread of being eaten, being cannibalized, a loss of a sense of the body from the encroachments of space, then different forms of space — corridors, rooms seen at expressionist angles, waste ground, empty spaces and empty roads, and the Falls as a black hole — would all imply different forms of nausea. Relation to that space, as in the speeded-up moments, implies something hyped up. In Buenos Aires, it is the cars that speed by fast, around the Obelisk. The centre of the city appears as a vortex, sucking things or people in. The vortex is repeated by the Iguazu Falls and increased by the circularity of the shot. The Obelisk and the Falls become the Scylla and Charbydis — devouring monster and sucking whirlpool — which are the two polarities of this Latin America. Similarly, in Taipei, the people are speeded up, rendered marionettes, under the new effects of speed in the mass rail transit system. A rail system intended to facilitate and speed things up has the reverse effect in making those who are its subjects into those who must hurry on down, or up, in a hysteric hyperintensity. Needless to say, this is the nearest to an image of Hong Kong that we get in the film; it is hardly necessary to imply that what is true of Taipei is true also of Hong Kong, since Taipei's MRT is an imitation of Hong Kong's MTR. The film finishes with the imitation. Wong Kar-wai's renderings of Hong Kong, seen in such a speeded-up way in *Fallen Angels*, a film whose distorted images have already been referred to, will come to mind, as will the double narratives of that film and of *Chungking Express*. It is as if the speed of the city forces upon the need to have dual and unrelated narratives: an aspect of its alienating power. *Happy Together* taps into this schizoid form of existence as a film and shows the symptoms that Lai and Ho have to endure. That they enjoy so many moments which are not quite melancholic, is something positive within the film.

8

Epilogue: *Happy Together* and *In the Mood for Love*

Wong Kar-wai's latest film to date is *In the Mood for Love* (2000), scripted by Wong with Chris Doyle and Mark Lee (photography), and Man Lim-chung and Alfred Yau (art directors) and William Chang (production designer). This film gives another context for *Happy Together* by centring on a couple, each married to other partners, who are older, middle-class and more financially secure than the characters in *Happy Together*. Mrs Chan (Maggie Cheung) and Mr Chow (Tony Leung) discover that each of their spouses is having an affair with the other's spouse. As in *Days of Being Wild*, the action is set in the past, beginning in Hong Kong in 1962 and then moving on to Singapore, where Chow goes in order to work in a newspaper office, and then finishing in French-ruled Cambodia in 1966. The Cambodia sequences use footage of Sihanouk greeting General De Gaulle at the airport outside Phomh Penh, and then showing Chow at the ruins of Angkor Wat, where the film ends. The linear plot and pace contrast with the speed and double narratives of *Chungking Express, Fallen Angels* and *Happy Together*.

The film's release coincided with the Merchant/Ivory film by Henry James, *The Golden Bowl* (1903), which has analogues in plot with *In the Mood for Love*. In *The Golden Bowl*, Adam Verver's wife, Charlotte Stant, is having an affair with a man named Amerigo who is in turn married to a woman named Maggie. Adam Verver and Maggie, who happen to be father and daughter from a previous marriage are thrown into a situation of emotional loss by their spouses' infidelity. In James's film, the question of what to do and how to behave, when there is the awareness of the possibility of behaviour becoming scandalous, is paramount. Danger springs from betrayals by people with whom trust cannot be broken. Such betrayal threatens the very sense of identity that the betrayed person has painfully built up for themselves in relation to their betrayer. It is the same situation in Wong Kar-wai's *Happy Together*, hence Lai's unhappiness which Chang detects. In this film, behaviour covers what runs unseen, below the public sphere. *In the Mood for Love*, like James's novel, focuses on the repressions that must take place for there to be a public sphere at all. So, in *Happy Together* Lai represses himself in order to work and Ho shows little repression at all until he is seen working, clearing up the flat and weeping when Lai has gone.

In the Mood for Love begins with the Chans and the Chows moving into rented accommodation next door to each other. The landlady (Rebecca Pan) eventually emigrates to the USA, fearful at what might be about to happen in Hong Kong: it is the year of the Cultural Revolution when anti-British riots occurred in Hong Kong. The theme of having no home is recognisable. Mr Chan is never seen though his voice is heard talking through a door offscreen, and Mrs Chow is only seen for a moment. Three-quarters of the way through the 1962 part of the film, it is apparent that they are in Japan together, Japan — a contrast to Argentina — being Hong Kong's 'other' in this film, with its fashions and luxury goods. The emphasis is on the couple left behind. At Mrs Chow's office, her boss (Lui Chun) is having an affair, and as part of her secretarial work, she must keep his mistress secret from his wife. Mr Chow works as a writer in an office where he listens to the things his colleague (Siu Ping-lam) gets up to in the local brothel. His hobby is writing martial arts serials — perhaps the script for *Ashes of Time* — almost the only way in which masculinity is inflected in the film.

In *In the Mood for Love* attention is drawn to social interrelationships through birthdays, indicators of continuity and of being happy together as well as signs of having an enduring relationship in an enduring place. In this film, everyone's birthday is marked by deception, the occasion of rich social comedy. The interchange of presents and doubling of presents (a tie, a handbag), marks the duplicity which adultery both requires and is produced by. The final irony is when Mr Chan wishes his wife a happy birthday on the radio, since he is away in Japan. The song he chooses to be played for her, a form of 'Happy Birthday', is Zhou Xuan's 'Huayang Nianhua', 'Full Bloom' — the Chinese title of the film, expressive of youth and the time for love. Eventually Mrs Chan and Mr Chow realise that their partners are together. They must now either become stylists of their own lives, creating their own narrative, or become like their partners. They play a game showing that 'we won't be like them'. They want to find out how the affair started and answer the question: Who made the first move?

In this activity, Mrs Chan and Mr Chow are slipping into the identity of the other partner; a husband imagining how his wife behaves and a wife her husband, in a chiastic mode. This is similar to the situation in *Happy Together* where Lai and Ho's identities are not stable, as in a moment referred to previously, when Ho is at the Bar Sur, Lai's workplace, and then he returns to the apartment after Lai has left and cleans up the apartment as if he were Lai. Identity is not singular but is, uncannily, shared. The risk the characters take is to be themselves and at the same time to find out what their partners think and say. The truly adulterous partners may be glimpsed in this other partnership; that they are both their identity and the identity of the others. Staging an affair, Mrs Chan and Mr Chow risk more than the unsuspected, adulterous pair, for people assume they *are* having an affair even though — as when they have to stay together one night because of a mahjong party taking place just outside their apartments where everyone would see that they had been together if they emerged from the room — they are doing nothing of the kind.

In this game they play roles, such as when Mrs Chan appears to confront her husband — at first, the audience would be convinced that it is indeed her husband, since he sits just out of camera and she faces him, but it becomes apparent that it is Chow — and asks him the question 'Do you have a mistress?' When Chow, speaking as her husband, admits it, she cannot hit him and it is apparent that this is because she is by now in love with Chow. She cannot believe in her own game. They repeat it but she weeps and says, 'I didn't expect it to hurt so much.' The self-fashioning they have tried, creating the self in a mode discussed by Foucault in *The Care of the Self*, has failed. Foucault describes an attempt to construct an ethics for the self, creating an 'aesthetics of existence' comparable to 'self-fashioning'.[1] They simulate adultery; ringing each other at work; he moves to a hotel and she visits him there, leaving things in the hotel — such as cigarette ends — which imply that they have been together. The device of entering and altering the apartment of someone you love appears in *As Tears Go By* and *Chungking Express*, where Faye Wong, in love with Cop 663, breaks into his apartment to clean it and decorate it; and in *Fallen Angels* with the agent of the killer. Ho plays a variant on it in cleaning up for Lai near the end of *Happy Together*. The game no longer works, however, *Happy Together* is not *Chungking Express*.

Maggie Cheung and Tony Leung attempt to rise above the narrative that has been given to them in *In the Mood for Love*.

Everything ends when he says, 'I thought we wouldn't be like them. But I was wrong. You won't leave your husband so I must go away.' She replies, 'I didn't think you'd fall in love with me.' To which he answers, 'I was only anxious to see how it started.' He adds, 'I thought I was in control,' but, 'feelings can creep up. Just like that.' Their belief in their identity betrays them. Tracing the narrative of their spouses to its origins pulls them into that narrative, which seduces them and makes them unable to act freely. *Happy Together* has no interest in origins — how Lai and Ho started becoming happy together — since Wong Kar-wai is not interested in the idea of people in Hong Kong being in a position to initiate something for themselves. This is the non-Hollywood aspect of his thought. Being caught in a narrative not of the subject's own making — which pulls Yuddy back into the past and destroys him — has political implications, for it raises the question: What chances of autonomous action are open to people in Hong Kong, so many of whom leave to 'start over'? As Ho and Lai in *Happy Together*, whose reaction to the way that events bear upon them is to think — perhaps unrealistically and hollowly — how they might 'start over', the characters of *In the Mood for Love* find they cannot go forward with their own narrative. Mrs Chan's unmarried name was Su Lizhen, the name of the woman Maggie Cheung played in *Days of Being Wild*. It is a film apparently intended to have a sequel: it finishes with the appearance of a gambler (Tony Leung), not seen before, in a sequence shot in a low-ceilinged room from a very cramped angle. Perhaps it is an image of the city's otherness because it contains so much more than can go into one narrative. Is Su Lizhen Mrs Chan two years later? Is Wong Kar-wai doubling the space of his own past by making this film as if it was a sequel to another fictional account of pre-modern Hong Kong? Perhaps the film is playing with origins where origins are only fictions.

Mr Chow transfers to Singapore. Four years later, they miss seeing each other at the old apartment in Hong Kong. She has a little boy; he is solitary. The action moves to Cambodia, where Mr Chow has been sent to cover de Gaulle's visit. Alone, he whispers his love-secret into the walls of Angkor Wat — following a recipe given to him in Singapore that if you must tell a secret, you should go up a mountain, find a tree, whisper into a hole in the tree, cover the hole with mud and leave the secret there. The act compares with Chang's desire in *Happy Together* to help Lai's unhappiness by dumping his sorrow at the end of the world. The romantic gesture is carried out with a sense of the inadequacy of the solution for the problem.

A similarity among the films is the displacement of location in both. Hong Kong, the setting for much of *In the Mood for Love,* is no more visible in that film than it was in *Happy Together*, and is different from the contemporary Hong Kong of *Chungking Express*. The apartments have the signs of Shanghainese culture and ways of living but no exterior shots define Hong Kong, though characters are seen standing against exterior walls. Offices are anonymous and the couple dine together outside in a Western-food restaurant — again, oddly displacing, especially with Spanish-sounding music played and sung by Nat King Cole, itself a faint reminder of Buenos Aires. In the same way *Days of Being Wild* uses Latino rhythms. The rest of the music, written by Michael Galasso, is equally Western in style, and the contrast with the Chinese 'happy birthday' song is strong. Anonymity increases with the hotel scenes. The atmosphere is claustrophobic and as exterior shots are often marked by rain, which stands in for weeping, and by British-looking taxis, the sense of a non-definable place is increased. Singapore is just as anonymously presented, though the film makes the place look poorer than Hong Kong and with less sense of a public infrastructure (as with the appearance of Manila in *Days of Being Wild*). The appearance of Cambodia at the end is dual. The appearance of de Gaulle at Phnom Penh echoes the reference to Deng near the end of *Happy Together*. Both world figures imply the relationship between the political and the emotional lives of people who are situated as they are because of the contingencies of power. In 1966, Hong Kong was doubly positioned in relation to Britain and the PRC, and Cambodia too, between France as the colonial power and the chain of events which were just about to follow with the Americans and the Khmer Rouge. To finish in the ruins of another empire, the Khmer, architects of Angkor Wat, is ironic. The history of South East Asia that is opened up by the date 1966 takes in significant and obvious shifts of power in Singapore, Cambodia, Hong Kong and mainland China which the characters have to live through (and casual reference is also made, in the 1966 sequences, to the Philippines). While there is no comparison between *Happy Together*'s Taiwan and Cambodia, except that both imply forms of exile and indifference to the individual (the same actor) wandering there, both imply displacement, a stalling of narrative. But Angkor Wat has no comparable significance to the Iguazu Falls which were desired and referred to by Lai and Ho and also by Chang, while nothing in *In the Mood for Love* implies desire for Angkor Wat. Instead, it is a reminder of a place with 'history', expressed in niches and corridors in the intricacies of the temple walls and, inside the doors, unprobed dark spaces which serve as places for memory. It is the antithesis to Hong Kong which presents, in comparison, a sense of flatness and apparent lack of history — but it seems that the film tries to give to the character of Hong Kong something of the architectural intricacy of Angkor Wat. Characters move into and emerge from the dark; they walk down dark corridors like the labyrinthine ones of *Happy Together*; often the image on the screen is of brilliant colour which appears as if in an epiphany out of the shadows which frame it. The bright colours of the varied cheongsams that Mrs Chan wears indicate the passage of time. The colours of the hotel's wallpaper with its purples, greens, dark reds, yellows and saffron all deepen Hong Kong's flatness. Repeated images of clocks and the use of telephones arouse thoughts of other places — more subtly than the image of a mobile phone might — which the camera brings into view as people are seen talking together on the phone, the camera swinging between them.

This attention to Hong Kong implies a further comparison with Henry James (who was also interested in how people become fascinated and haunted by the identity of another, trying to analyse it from rooms and furnishings and, finally, taking it over). James, as a postcolonial writer, left the United States with the sense that the place had no past that could be used to construct the present. He believed that the lack of history would disable America's attempt to produce any literature. But he knew that this was not enough as a response and in *The Jolly Corner* (1908) he imagines a character returning to New York after 20 years away and wondering if he can find the ghost of his alternative self, the self that would have been had he stayed in America.[2] Wong Kar-wai's films set in the 1960s are motivated by the desire to find a ghost; to locate in the past another possibility, denied by the facts. In a different way, *Happy Together* doubles the space of Hong Kong by setting the action in Buenos Aires, an unknowable space, where a history can be written — as Borges wrote the history of the tango, for instance, which works as a counter-history to U.S. imperial history. Wong Kar-wai's films about Hong Kong seem to me like James's attempts to write about America at a time when no one took the idea of American literature seriously, and as James treated Europe as a way to discuss America, so Wong Kar-wai uses Buenos Aires, a place with much to say to Hong Kong.

In the Mood for Love brings out another fascination in Wong Kar-wai, the ability of curtains, veils and fabrics to give depth and forms of concealment, which appeared in the curtain moving before the face of the swordsman Ouyang Feng in *Ashes of Time* and was also apparent in the curtains blowing in the apartment at Buenos Aires in *Happy Together*, which were uncannily associated with the absence of Ho. Cigarette smoke, associated with Mr Chow, at several points acts like a veil. At one point a window hung with curtains is seen, behind these, net curtains, and behind these, a Venetian blind. Derrida writing on Nietzsche in *Spurs: Nietzsche's Styles* links a fascination with the veil with a feminine concealment or withdrawal which for Derrida and for Nietzsche is the antithesis of the will to truth — that which makes truth flat, singular and unitary in character.[3] The veil as text(ile) doubles space and makes truth plural, unknowable save in momentary flashes which also conceal it. Such veils appearing here are places for memory to haunt, and they make 1960s Hong Kong a strangely evocative place. Wong Kar-wai has returned to a past layered with the present, enriching present-day Hong Kong with the sense that it might have had such a past. Characters move and define themselves against an aesthetic sensuousness, which implies that their ethics of existence is a form of aesthetics; that aesthetics is enriching. In *Happy Together*, the kitsch lamp of the Iguazu Falls, which Lai quite unaffectedly says he likes, and which was given to him by Ho, is similar in effect. It is a form of art defined by colour whose interest grows and literally illuminates the apartment, and does much to keep Lai and Ho together. At the end, Ho restores it and it plays its part in giving depth to his memories of Lai. And because of it, when Lai reaches the Falls he says, 'I thought of Po-wing.'

The places of memory are not at any stage in Wong Kar-wai's films the public *lieux de memoires* discussed by Pierre Nora[4] — they are not to do with a history which could be memorialized or celebrated in monuments. Angkor Wat as a monument and tourist site exists in the film as a place which has *no* association with any character or event in the film. The film constructs a secret and alternative history — giving expression to the secret which is whispered into the walls of Angkor Wat — by suggesting that there are ghosts which double the space of Hong Kong; people whose lives mean that if they were 30 in 1962, they would be now at the time of the film's making, part of another Hong Kong to which all their adult lives had contributed. At the end, words from a Chinese text appear on the screen: 'He remembers those vanished years as though looking though a dirty window-pane. The past is something he could see but not touch and everything he sees is blurred and indistinct.' Mr Chow at the end walks away from Angkor Wat, a place of a past which has been home to a thousand incidents, public and private. His black suit indicates perhaps mournfulness or melancholia, which fits with *Happy Together*, but his past is now incorporated into the history that Angkor Wat, itself about to go through scenes of violence, preserves. The confessional act, if it is that, has had its effect. Perhaps it is hardly confessional, but rather an assertion of his own history.

The use of the Chinese text at first and last replaces a typical Wong Kar-wai device — the voice-over. The voice-over in earlier films — most strikingly in *Ashes of Time*, where it is positively garrulous — divides the narrative from the image, in that fracturing noticed earlier in discussing allegory. Its absence here is signalled by the device of the secret being told silently, unlike Lai's audible sobs into the tape recorder. The suspension of a voice-over is a move away from narrative and the past and throws emphasis onto the present. In this way, the film keeps aloof from any sentimentality, and this is different from *Happy Together*. The film is not violent, even if Angkor Wat implies a violent history. To recall the repeated aggression in the relation of Lai and Ho, including the violence of the language used in argument, makes the point that the director's interests have moved on. Violence, as Lacan implies in his essay on 'Aggressivity in Psychoanalysis' (*Ecrits*), may respond to a failure in the other to sustain the narcissism the subject requires, or a failure in the subject to be able to maintain narcissism, which requires lashing out at the other. This film implies people who keep a certain narcissism, which the film also maintains in its colours and shapes, and in the curves and enclosed spaces in which characters are ringed and picked out by the camera. The preservation of narcissism shows its independence, its aloofness from present or past Hong Kong; it is self-fashioning, akin to certain potentialities in Chang's character in *Happy Together*. He too, keeps an aloof quality which means that he is never associated with violence, and the causes of this cannot necessarily be reduced to what Lai says: that Chang has a home. But the title *Happy Together* implies a failure of narcissism and emphasises the melancholia which underlies the later film.

The gay relationship is no allegory of the later film's heterosexual one; no generalisations are possible about a pair in love, except that one pair in love may contain the identities of another pair in love. *Happy Together* is enriched by *In the Mood for Love*, but the latter film simplifies nothing in it, letting it stand as, in my belief, Wong Kar-wai's most thought-provoking film, demanding an enlargement of the critic's modes of thinking through which to consider it.

Notes

Chapter 1   Introduction: Approaching the Film

1   On this film see Ackbar Abbas, *Hong Kong: Culture and the Politics of Disappearance* (Hong Kong: Hong Kong University Press, 1997), pp. 34–6. See pp. 48–62 for discussion of later films, not including *Happy Together*.

2   Christopher Doyle has written about making the film in *Don't Try for Me Argentina* (Hong Kong: City Entertainment, 1997).

3   A useful discussion of Wong Kar Wai appears in David Bordwell, *Planet Hong Kong: Cinema and the Art of Entertainment* (Cambridge, Mass.: Harvard University Press, 2000), pp. 270–89. See also Tony Rayns, 'Poet of Time', *Sight and Sound* (September 1995): 12–4; Larry Gross, 'Nonchalant Grace', *Sight and Sound* (September 1996): 6–10; Tony Rayns, 'Charisma Express', *Sight and Sound* (January 2000): 34–6; Tony Rayns, 'In the Mood for Edinburgh', *Sight and Sound* (August 2000): 14–7.

4   This is a reference to the essay by J. L. Borges, 'Kafka and his Precursors', *Non-Fiction 1922–1986,* ed. Eliot Weinberger (Harmondsworth: Penguin, 2001), pp. 363–5.

Chapter 2 *Happy Together* and Allegory

1   Fredric Jameson, 'Third-World Literature in the Era of Multinational Capitalism', *Social Text* 15 (1986): 65–88; quotations taken from pp. 67 and 69.

2   Aijaz Ahmad, *In Theory: Classes, Nations, Literatures* (London: Verso, 1992), pp. 95–122.

3   Gayatri Chakravorty Spivak, *A Critique of Postcolonial Reason: Toward a History of the Vanishing Present* (Cambridge, Mass.: Harvard University Press, 1999), p. 208.

4   Italo Calvino, *Invisible Cities*, trans. William Weaver (New York: Harcourt Brace and Co., 1974), pp. 68–9. The citation here omits the italics into which the whole passage is put.

5   Lisa Odham Stokes and Michael Hoover, *City on Fire: Hong Kong Cinema* (London: Verso, 1999), pp. 268–79.

6   Walter Benjamin, *The Origin of German Tragic Drama,* trans. John Osborne (London: Verso, 1977), p. 175.

7   Paul de Man, 'The Rhetoric of Temporality' in *Blindness and Insight: Essays in the Rhetoric of Contemporary Criticism* (Second Edition: London: Routledge, 1983), p. 207.

8   Paul de Man, 'The Concept of Irony', in *Aesthetic Ideology*, ed. Andrzej Warminski (Minneapolis: University of Minnesota Press, 1996), p. 179. The translator adds in a footnote something from de Man's lecture-notes: 'irony is (permanent) parabasis of allegory — intelligibility of (representational) narrative disrupted at all times.'

9   Foucault, Introduction to *Folie et Déraison: L'Histoire de la Folie à l'Age Classique* (Paris: Libraire Plon, 1961), p. v. Not in the English translation.

10   It is relevant to recall his role as the possibly homosexual Peking opera singer in Chen Kaige's film of 1993, *Farewell My Concubine*; where his role is someone who cannot distinguish between art and life, but plays himself all the time. That may be the subject of a trope in *Happy Together*, where, in parodic fashion, he may be acting himself. Audrey Yue suggests that Leslie Cheung acts in a self-parodic mode, and thus '"queers" what is essentially a straight film,' Audrey Yue, in '"What's so Queer About *Happy Together*?" a.k.a. Queer(N)Asian: Interface,

Community, Belonging', *Inter-Asia Cultural Studies* 1.2 (2000): 251–264, p. 254.

Chapter 3   Contexts: Why Buenos Aires?

1   For a reading of the city, see Jason Wilson, *Buenos Aires: A Cultural and Literary Companion* (Oxford: Signal Books, 1999): a guidebook aware of *Happy Together*.
2   V. S. Naipaul, *The Return of Eva Perón* (Harmondsworth: Penguin, 1981), pp. 93–164.
3   I take this point from Marta E. Savigliano, *Tango and the Political Economy of Passion* (Boulder, Colorado: Westview Press, 1995), p. 22–3.
4   Bordwell, p. 272. Alejo Carpentier, *The Kingdom of This World*, trans. Harriet de Onís (London: Andre Deutsch, 1990) Prologue, no page numbers given. The Spanish phrase is 'lo real maravilloso' — the marvellous in the real.
5   Jorge Luis Borges, *The Total Library: Non-Fiction 1922–1986* (Harmondsworth: Penguin, 2001), p. 432.
6   Borges, p. 426.
7   Its Chinese title is the same as the Chinese title for *Happy Together*.
8   *City on Fire* suggests *Heartbreak Tango* (1969) as a model, but though I think it is, it is hardly for the reasons given: 'the story of a son discovering his father's gay lover' (p. 269) — this is not the plot of *Heartbreak Tango*.
9   Manuel Puig, *Kiss of the Spider Woman,* trans. Thomas Kolchie (London: Arena, 1984). For guidance on Puig's novels, see Lucille Kerr, *Suspended Fictions: Reading Novels by Manuel Puig* (Urbana: University of Illinois Press, 1987).
10   Manuel Puig, *The Buenos Aires Affair*, trans. Suzanne Jill Levine (London: Faber, 1989), pp. 83–7.
11   Manuel Puig, *Heartbreak Tango: A Serial*, trans. Suzanne Jill Levine (London: Arena, 1987). In Spanish the title was *Boquitas pintadas* — 'painted little lips' — a quotation from a tango written by Alfredo Le Pera and sung by Carlos Gardel.

12   Cortazar's short story, 'Return Trip Tango' might also have resonances as a title for *Happy Together*. It comes from a volume celebrating the mythicizing of another film actress, this time Glenda Jackson, not Rita Hayworth: *We Love Glenda So Much and Other Stories*, trans. Gregory Rabasa (New York: Knopf, 1983).

13   For this point see Pamela Bacarisse, *Impossible Choices: The Implications of the Cultural References in the Novels of Manuel Puig* (Calgary: University of Calgary Press, 1993), p. 19.

14   Naipaul, pp. 148–51.

Chapter 4   Contexts: The Road Movie

1   Jorge Luis Borges, *The Aleph and Other Stories 1933–1969*, trans. Norman Thomas di Giovanni (New York: Picador Books, 1971), p. 120. The story relates to another, 'Man on Pink Corner', in *A Universal History of Infamy* (1935) which is about one of the poorest areas of Buenos Aires (Palermo) and another evocation of the tango and masculinity. Both stories can be found in *Collected Fictions*, trans. Andrew Hurley (Harmondsworth: Penguin, 1998).

2   Eve Kosofsky Sedgwick, *Between Men: English Literature and Male Homosocial Desire* (New York: Collumbia University Press, 1985).

3   Timothy Corrigan, *A Cinema Without Walls: Movies and Culture After Vietnam* (London: Routledge, 1991), pp. 137–60.

4   Quoted by Steven Cohan from Sharon Willis in *The Road Movie Book*, ed. Steven Cohan and Ina Rae Hark (London: Routledge, 1997), p. 12.

5   The point is made by Bennet Schaber in *The Road Movie Book*, p. 42.

Chapter 5   Reading the Film

1   Manuel Puig, *Betrayed By Rita Hayworth*, trans. Suzanne Jill Levine (New York: Vintage, 1971), p. 173.

2   Rey Chow, 'Nostalgia of the New Wave: Structure in Wong Kar-wai's

Happy Together', *Camera Obscura: Feminism, Culture and Media Studies* 42 (September 1999): 31–49.

3   See the study by Gerald Martin, *Journeys Through the Labyrinth: Latin American Fiction in the Twentieth Century* (London: Verso, 1989).

4   On the irrationality of so many of Wong Kar-wai's characters, see Ewa Mazierska and Laura Rascaroli, 'Trapped in the Present: Time in the Films of Wong Kar-wai', *Film Criticism* (25 Winter 2000–2001): 2–20.

5   Suzanne Jill Levine, *Manuel Puig and the Spider Woman* (New York: Farrar, Strauss and Giroux, 2000), p. 405; see also pp. 210–7.

6   'A History of the Tango', in Borges, p. 396, earlier, p. 395.

7   For Piazzolla, see Maria Susana Azzi and Simon Collier, *Le Grand Tango: The Life and Music of Astor Piazzolla* (Oxford: Oxford University Press, 2000). They discuss other members of the band: such as the Uruguayan pianist Pablo Zinger, the Cuban saxophonist Paquito D'Rivera, the Argentine guitarist Rodolpho Alchourron. Others playing were Fernando Suarez Paz and Andy Gonzalez.

8   For the significance of yellow, see my *Lost in the American City: Dickens, James, Kafka* (New York: Palgrave, 2001), pp. 14–6.

9   Arthur Rimbaud, *Les Illuminations* in *Collected Poems* (Harmondsworth: Penguin, 1962), pp. 254–5. My translation.

10   See Donald S. Castro, *The Argentine Tango as Social History, 1880–1955* (San Francisco: Mellen Research University Press, 1990), p. 175.

11   For discussion of this poem, see Ross Chambers, *The Writing of Melancholy: Modes of Opposition in Early French Modernism* trans. Mary Seidman Trouville (Chicago: University of Chicago Press, 1993): and see this book also for discussions of melancholia (see chapter 7 notes).

12   On these points, see Eduardo P. Archetti, *Masculinities: Football, Polo and the Tango in Argentina* (Oxford: Berg, 1999); see p. 46 for the date, and pp. 182–9 for Maradona.

13   Rimbaud, pp. 255–6.

14   I refer to Freud, *Beyond the Pleasure Principle* in *The Penguin Freud vol. 11* (Harmondsworth: Penguin, 1977), pp. 283–7.

15   See Wilson, pp. 205–7.

16   Quoted from Luis Roldan, 'Blame that Tango' in Puig, *Heartbreak Tango*, p. 45. Savigliano (p. 57) translates it as 'Maldito Tango', as follows: 'Blame it on that cursed tango/that my lover taught me to dance/ and that later mired me in the mud.' She cites it as composed by Osman Pérez Freyre in 1918.

17   Bordwell, p. 272.

Chapter 6   *Happy Together* and Homosexuality

1   For discussion of this film, see *City on Fire*, p. 85 and *Planet Hong Kong*, pp. 153–4.

2   For this film and its sequel, *Who's the Woman, Who's the Man?* (1996) see *City on Fire*, pp. 229–37.

3   For masculinity: see Norman Bryson, 'Gericault and Masculinity' in Norman Bryson, Michael Ann Holly and Keith Moxey (eds.) *Visual Culture: Images and Interpretations* (Hanover, NH: University Press of New England, 1994), pp. 228–59.

4   Foucault barely discusses lesbianism, and leaves it open how his account could be applied there. My silence on it here relates to this and to the content of the film.

5   On this film, see Phillip Brian Harper, ' "The Subversive Edge": *Paris is Burning*, Social Critique and the Limits of Subjective Agency', *Diacritics* 24 (1994): 90–103.

6   Quoted, *City on Fire,* p. 275

7   Lacan's discussion of the symbolic order, derived from his reading of Levi-Strauss, appears 'The Function and Field of Speech and Language in Psychoanalysis', *Ecrits: A Selection*, trans. Alan Sheridan (London: Tavistock, 1977), pp. 61–6.

8   Bisexuality seems to be at the heart of psychoanalysis: see Freud, 'the motive force of repression in each individual is a struggle between the two sexual characters. The dominant sex of the person, that which is the more strongly developed, has repressed the mental representation of the subordinated sex into the unconscious' — 'A Child is Being Beaten', *On Psychopathology: The Penguin Freud* 10 (Harmondsworth: Penguin, 1979), p. 188. This suggests an

undifferentiated sexual nature prior to entry into language (identifiable, for Freud, with the Oedipal phase), but in Lacan things are different. Male and female positions are both existent within a symbolic order which defines male and female alike in relation to the phallus, so that desire does not coincide with gender positions as defined there. 'The vacillation psychoanalytic experience reveals in the subject regarding his masculine or feminine being is not so much related to his biological bisexuality as to the fact that there is nothing in his dialectic that represents the bipolarity of sex' — as there perhaps cannot be when both sexes are so defined. 'Position of the Unconscious' in *Reading Seminar XI: Lacan's Four Fundamental Concepts of Psychoanalysis*, ed. Bruce Fink, Richard Feldsten and Maire Jaanus (Albany: SUNY, 1995), p. 276. There Lacan says 'there is no access to the opposite sex as Other' in the symbolic order, and Fink adds (p. 280) that this could also be translated as 'the Other of the opposite sex'.

9   Jacques Lacan, 'On a Question Preliminary to any Possible Treatment of Psychosis', *Ecrits*, p. 200.

10 Jacques Derrida, 'Le Facteur de la Vérité', in *The Postcard: From Socrates to Freud and Beyond*, trans. Alan Bass (Chicago: University of Chicago Press, 1987), pp. 479–80. It is Derrida's critique of Lacan's reading of Poe's 'The Purloined Letter'. See the discussion by Barbara Johnson, 'The Frame of Reference: Poe, Lacan, Derrida', in Robert Young (ed.) *Untying the Text: A Post-Structuralist Reader* (London: Routledge, 1981), pp. 225–43.

11 Lacan's Seminar XX ('God and the *Jouissance* of the Woman: A Love Letter' in *Feminine Sexuality*, ed. Juliet Mitchell and Jacqueline Rose [London: Macmillan, 1982], pp. 137–61) and the seminar of 21 January 1975 (seminar XXII) discusses most the question of the 'otherness' of the feminine; that this does not enter into phallocentric discourse.

12 Freud, 'On the Universal Tendency to Debasement in the Sphere of Love', *The Penguin Freud: vol 7: On Sexuality* (Harmondsworth: Penguin, 1977), p. 258.

13 Michel Foucault, *The History of Sexuality*, trans. Robert Hurley (Harmondsworth: Penguin, 1981), p. 59.

14 Chow, p. 41.

Chapter 7 *Happy Together*, Hong Kong and Melancholy

1   'Compulsory Heterosexuality and Lesbian Existence' (1980) in *Adrienne Rich's Poetry and Prose*, ed. Barbara Charlesworth Gelpi and Albert Gelpi (New York: W.W. Norton, 1983), pp. 203–23.

2   Quoted, Pamela Bacarisse, *The Necessary Dream: A Study of the Novels of Manuel Puig* (Yotowa, NJ.: Barnes and Noble, 1988), p. 37. Bacarisse also quotes Sábato that the tango is 'often accompanied by desperation, rancour, threats and sarcasm' (p. 240) — features of resentment.

3   Quoted in Marta E. Savigliano, *Tango and the Political Economy of Passion* (Boulder; Westview Press, 1995), p. 45.

4   The expression of Harley Dean Oberhelman, *Ernesto Sábato* (Boston: Twayne, 1970), p. 45.

5   Chow, p. 45.

6   Chow, p. 44.

7   Bordwell, pp. 280–1.

8   Octavio Paz, *The Labyrinth of Solitude: Life and Thought in Mexico*, trans. Lysander Kemp (New York: Grove Press, 1961), p. 203.

9   Freud, 'Mourning and Melancholia', *The Penguin Freud vol. 11* (Harmondsworth: Penguin, 1977), p. 254.

10   Fredric Jameson discusses nostalgia in this way in *Postmodernisn, Or the Cultural Logic of Late Capitalism* (London: Verso, 1991), p. 19.

11   Ackbar Abbas, 'The Erotics of Disappointment,' in *Wong Kar Wai* (Paris: Dis Voir, 1998), 39–81; pp. 45, 46.

12   Walter Benjamin, *Illuminations*, trans. Harry Zohn (London: Jonathan Cape, 1970), p. 263.

13   Roger Caillois, 'Mimicry and Legendary Psychasthenia', trans. John Shepherd, *October 31* (1984): 17–31 (p. 30).

14   Stuart C. Aitken and Christopher Lee Lukinbeal in *The Road Movie Book*, p. 369.

Chapter 8   Epilogue: *Happy Together* and *In the Mood for Love*

1   Michel Foucault, *The Use of Pleasure: The History of Sexuality vol. 2*, trans. Robert Hulery (Harmondsworth: Penguin, 1987), p. 11.

2   See my *Henry James: Critical Issues* (London: Macmillan, 2000) for these issues.

3   Jacques Derrida, *Spurs: Nietzsche's Styles*, trans. Barbara Harlow (Chicago: University of Chicago Press, 1979).

4   Pierre Nora, *Realms of Memory: Rethinking the French Past*, ed. Lawrence Kritzman and trans. Arthur Goldhammer (New York: Columbia University Press, 1996), 3 vols.

Filmography

Happy Together/Chunguang Zhaxie (春光乍洩)

Hong Kong 1997

Director
Wong Kar-wai

Producer
Wong Kar-wai

Screenplay
Wong Kar-wai

Director of Photography
Christopher Doyle

Editors
William Chang Suk-ping
Wong Ming-lam

Production Designer
William Chang Suk-ping

Music
Danny Chung

Production Companies
Block 2 Pictures Inc. in association with Prenom H Co. Ltd./Seawoo Film
Co. Ltd. presents a Jet Tone Production

Executive Producer
Chan Ye-cheng

Associate Producers
Hiroko Shinohara
Chung T. J.
Christopher Tseng Ching-chao

Production Supervisor
Jacky Pang Yee-wah

Production Co-ordinator
Joseph Chi Chiong-Chavez

Unit Production Manager
Chang Hsien-jen

Assistant Director
Johnnie Kong Yeuk-shing

Visual Continuity
Carmen Lui Lai-wah

Make-up
Kwan Lee-na

Music Editor
Tang Siu-lam

Soundtrack
'Cucurrucucu Paloma' by Tomas Mendez, arranged by Jacques Morelenbaum, performed by Caetano Veloso; 'Chunga's Revenge' by Frank Zappa, performed by Frank Zappa, Ian Underwood, Sugar Cane Harris, Max Bennett and Aynsley Dunbar; 'I Have Been in You' by Frank Zappa, performed by Frank Zappa, Adrian Belew, Tommy Mars, Peter Wolf, Patrick O'Hearn, Terry Bozzio, Ed Mann, Napoleon M. Brock, Andre Lewis, Randy Thornton and Davey Moire; 'Prologue (Tango Apasionada)', 'Finale (Tango Apasionada)' by/arranged by Astor Piazzola, performed by Astor Piazzola, Pablo Zinger, Fernando Suarez Paz, Paquito D'Rivera, Andy Gonzalez and Radolfo Alchourron; 'Happy Together' by Garry Bonner and Alan Gordon, arranged/performed by Danny Chung

Sound Recording
Leung Chi-tat

Sound Editor
Tu Duu-chih

Cast

Leslie Cheung Kwok-wing (張國榮)	as Ho Po-wing (何寶榮)
Tong Leung Chiu-wai (梁朝偉)	as Lai Yiu-fai (黎耀輝)
Chang Chen (張震)	as Chang (小張)

Certificate
15

Distributor
Artificial Eye

8,734 feet

97 minutes 3 seconds

Dolby

In Colour Subtitles

Bibliography

General:

Abbas, Ackbar. *Hong Kong: Culture and the Politics of Disappearance.*
Hong Kong: Hong Kong University Press, 1997.

Abbas, Ackbar, Lalanne, Jean-Marc, Martinez, David, & Ngai, Jimmy.
Wong Kar Wai. Paris: Dis Voir, 1997.

Berry, Chris, ed. *Perspectives on Chinese Cinema.* London: British Film
Institute, 1991.

Bordwell, David. *Planet Hong Kong: Popular Cinema and the Art of
Entertainment.* Cambridge: Harvard University Press, 2000.

Dannen, Fredric, & Long, Barry. *Hong Kong Babylon: An Insider's Guide
to the Hollywood of the East.* London & Boston: Faber and Faber,
1997.

Gross, Larry. 'Nonchalant Grace.' *Sight and Sound* (September 1996)
6 (9): 6–9.

Hampton, Howard. 'Blur as Genre.' *Artforum International* (March 1996)
34 (7): 91–4.

Hoover, Michael, & Stokes, Lisa Odham. *City on Fire: Hong Kong Cinema.*
London & New York: Verso, 1999.

Huang, Tsung-Yi. 'Hong Kong Blue: Flâneurie with the Camera's Eye in a Phantasmagoric Global City.' *Journal of Narrative Theory* (Fall 2000) 30 (3): 385–402.

Law, Jo. 'Wong Kar-Wai's Cinema.' *Metro* (Summer 2001) 126: 92–7.

Lilley, Rozanna. *Staging Hong Kong: Gender and Performance in Transition.* Hawaii: University of Hawaii Press, 1998.

Ong, Han. 'Wong Kar-Wai.' *BOMB* (Winter 1998) 62: 48–54.

Phelan, Shane, & Stychin, Carl F., eds. *A Nation by Rights: National Cultures, Sexual Identity Politics, and the Discourse of Rights.* Pennsylvania: Temple University Press, 1998.

Rayns, Tony. 'Poet of Time.' *Sight and Sound* (September 1995) 5 (9): 12–6.

———. 'Charisma Express.' *Sight and Sound* (Jan 2000) 10 (1): 34–6.

Rosenbaum, Jonathan. *Moving Places: A Life at the Movies.* California: University of California Press, 1995.

Stephens, Chuck. 'Time Pieces.' *Film Comment* (Jan/Feb 1996) 32 (1): 12–8.

Tang, Denise. 'Popular Dialogues of a "Discreet" Nature.' *Asian Cinema* (Fall 1998) 10 (1): 198–207.

Teo, Stephen. *Hong Kong Cinema: The Extra Dimensions.* London: British Film Institute, 1997.

———. 'The 1970s: Movement and Transition.' In *The Cinema of Hong Kong: History, Arts, Identity*, edited by David Desser & Poshek Fu. Cambridge: Cambridge University Press, 2000.

Tsui, Curtis K. 'Subjective Culture and History: the Ethnographic Cinema of Wong Kar-Wai.' *Asian Cinema* (Winter 1995) 7 (2): 93–124.

Yau, Esther C. M. (Ed.) *At Full Speed: Hong Kong Cinema in a Borderless World.* Minnesota: University of Minnesota Press, 2001.

Yeh, Yueh-Yu. 'A Life of Its Own: Musical Discourses in Wong Kar-Wai's Films.' *Post-Script: Essays in Film and the Humanities* (Fall 1999) 19 (1): 120–36.

Zhou, Juanita-Huan. 'Ashes of Time: The Tragedy and Salvation of the Chinese Intelligentsia.' *Asian Cinema* (Fall 1998) 10 (1): 62–70.

On *Happy Together*:

Barry, Chris. 'Happy Alone? Sad Young Men in East Asian Gay Cinema.' *Journal of Homosexuality* (2000) 39 (3–4): 187–200.

Chow, Rey. 'Nostalgia of the New Wave: Structure in Wong Kar-Wai's *Happy Together*' *Camera Obscura: A Journal of Feminism, Culture, and Media Studies* (September 1999) 42: 31–48.

Davidson, Nina. 'Wong Kar-wai Tackles Controversy in *Happy Together*.' *Hollywood Online* 4 (30 November 1997). http://www.hollywood.co/news/topstories/11–04–97/html/2–2.html.

Doyle, Christopher. *Don't Try for Me Argentina*. Hong Kong: City Entertainment, 1997.

He Wai-Jian. '*Chun Guan Zha Xie* Zai Xie Chun Guan' (Xun Zhao Zero Degree Country). *City Entertainment* 545 (Mar 2000), p. 71.

Li Zhuo-Tao. 'Jiu Qi Gang Pian De Jiu Qi Qin Huai.' *Hong Kong Panorama 97–98: The 22nd Hong Kong International Film Festival*. Hong Kong: The Provisional Urban Council of Hong Kong, 1998, 14–6.

Rayns, Tony. 'To the End of the World.' *Sight and Sound* (May 1997) 7 (5): 14–7.

Yue, Audrey. 'What's So Queer about *Happy Together*? a.k.a. Queer (N)Asian: Interface, Community, Belonging.' *Inter-Asia Cultural Studies* (2000) 1 (2): 251–64.

On *In the Mood for Love*:

Cooper, Dennis. 'Mood Swing.' *Artforum International* (Feb 2001) 39 (6): 41– 5.

Jones, Kent. 'Of Love and the City.' *Film Comment* (Jan/Feb 2001) 37 (1): 22–5.

Rayns, Tony. 'In the Mood for Edinburgh.' *Sight and Sound* (Aug 2000) 10 (8): 14–7.

Interviews:

'Happy Talk.' *Village Voice* (Oct 1997) 42: 85–9.
'Home Is Where the Heart Is: Wong Kar-Wai and Christopher Doyle on
    *Happy Together.' Hong Kong Panorama 97–98: The 22nd Hong Kong
    International Film Festival,* pp. 30–5. Hong Kong: The Provisional
    Urban Council of Hong Kong, 1998.
'It's Nostalgia in the Future.' *Newsweek* (Atlantic Edition) (May 2001) 137
    (21): 60–3.